PRAISE FOR *FEMALE BREADWINNERS*:

'Employers: ignore this at your peril; this is vital to companies'
understanding of how to retain top-performing, senior women.'
CAROL PATERSON SMITH, CEO, www.AlphaFemaleClub.com

'A must-read for every 21st century household.'
MERRYN SOMERSET-WEBB, Editor in Chief, MoneyWeek

'A wonderfully written follow-up to Beyond the Boys' Club
and a must-have book for female breadwinners.'
MAGGIE BERRY, MD, www.womenintechnology.co.uk

'This book gives us thought-provoking insight into the emerging
new world, one in which we as women take more direct control as
earners but in which true equilibrium will need both men and women
to face up to what their own identity means in the 21st century and
how to get comfortable in that skin. To be read by men and women,
a trusted companion for modern families across the globe.'
BARBARA-ANN KING
Director of SmartWoman and Head of Investments, Barclay Wealth

'Once again Suzanne eloquently lifts the lid on yet another
taboo subject. In doing so, she has generated an insightful and
intriguing expo into the complex world of the female breadwinner.
A fantastic read, and once again another book from Suzanne that
I will continue to recommend for years to come.'
VANESSA VALLELY, MD, www.wearethecity.com

'Suzanne plots a way forward that makes more sense
for women – and men. As such, this book is at heart about
helping all of us be better…better people.'
ADAM QUINTON, Gender & Policy Program at the
School of International & Public Affairs, Columbia University

D0237830

SUZANNE DOYLE-MORRIS, PhD

FEMALE BREADWINNERS

HOW THEY MAKE
RELATIONSHIPS WORK
AND WHY THEY ARE
THE FUTURE OF THE
MODERN WORKFORCE

WIT & WISDOM PRESS

For my husband Geoff

PUBLISHED BY WIT & WISDOM PRESS

ISBN 978-0-9562688-1-5

Designed and typeset by Julia Lloyd Design
Printed and bound by Lightning Source

2 4 6 8 10 9 7 5 3 1

Mixed Sources
Product group from well-managed forests, controlled sources and recycled wood or fiber
www.fsc.org Cert no. SW-COC-004900
© 1996 Forest Stewardship Council
FSC

CONTENTS

INTRODUCTION

WHY FOCUS ON FEMALE
BREADWINNERS?

*'Most men have learned to enjoy loving a doer
rather than a dodo.'*

HELEN GURLEY BROWN

Several months ago, I had three separate conversations in a single day that inspired me to write a book on the rise of the female breadwinner. Those three conversations illustrated that women functioning as primary breadwinners is an increasingly common, but also complex, phenomenon emerging in the modern workplace and in personal relationships. Three conversations were enough to convince me there was a real story to tell.

It was an unseasonably warm spring day in London, and I was scheduled for executive coaching sessions with three completely different women. At the first session, Clara, an executive for a global pharmaceutical company, had been approached about a promotion to a 'Head of Country' role. The job offer was a real step up for her, and a great indication of the potential her boss saw in her. However, the opportunity meant relocating to Finland.

As we talked, Clara said: 'Naturally, I'll have to talk it over with my husband, Richard. Even though he works from home as an IT consultant, and so could probably continue his work, I want to make this a completely equal decision. I certainly wouldn't be here without him.' Richard worked part-time and fitted his work around the schedules of their two small boys.

In our sessions, Clara had always mentioned with pride the support Richard gave for her high-earning role and how good he was with their sons. Clara was clearly very reliant and grateful for the flexibility.

My next session was with Kylie, a project manager for an IT firm. She spoke of her desire to move into the non-profit sector. Kylie explained: 'I'd like to be using my organisational skills for a better cause. Don't get me wrong, I love my colleagues; but I'd like to try working for a charity or maybe in the education sector.' This was a topic that had come up before, but Kylie was hesitant about making the switch.

The reason for her hesitation? She earned well in the IT sector and was the primary breadwinner for the family. Her husband, Nathan, worked in science education for a national museum, bringing in less than half her salary. She sighed: 'I'm so pleased Nathan works in a field he loves. But on my down days or when I am considering anything new for myself, I can't get away from the fact that our household income is pretty much my responsibility. A move to the charitable sector would almost inevitably halve my salary.'

After a pensive lunch thinking about the issues these women faced, I travelled to my last session to see Raina, who worked at an investment bank. She was delighted to talk, enthusiastically saying the coaching work we'd already done together had paid off! After holding her ground in negotiations, and asking for more than she would have accepted, she was awarded a larger bonus than anticipated.

In passing, she mentioned: 'I need to be careful about how excited I am when I tell my fiancé, Rafiq. I know he's proud of my achievements, but I think he feels slightly threatened by the fact I earn so well.'

Raina and Rafiq had met on an MBA programme. While she had gone straight into financial services, he had recently set up a small start-up consultancy. She continued: 'His company isn't growing at the pace he would have liked and I think he feels slightly competitive with me. No doubt, he'll be happy I'm bringing home more money. But there will be a small part of him that will resent that it's not *him* bringing it in.'

What struck me from these three conversations was how each woman was the primary breadwinner for her family. In our sessions it had never been raised as a main issue, but it often lurked in the background affecting how the women relied on their partners, their internal sense of responsibility and their career choices.

In fact, I knew this was a topic worth exploring when I looked through my list of clients later that night. With only one or two exceptions, my female clients were *all* women who out-earned their husbands, partners and boyfriends.

Clearly, being the main breadwinner is an expectation most men have contended with for generations. What is noteworthy *now* is how many women in heterosexual partnerships today carry both the burden and the advantages this role brings. These women's experiences demonstrate how the role challenges many of the societal expectations with which we were raised.

Even more interestingly, both women and men who are progressive, and I would even say feminist in their outlook towards these changing modern roles, still find negotiating them within their *own* relationships to be a challenge. It can be equally difficult to reconcile yourself to a role you didn't anticipate – whether as breadwinner or not. Their male partner's reactions to these non-traditional roles ran from support and pride to resentment and competitiveness. And in no way was this range of emotion an exclusively male phenomenon; the women themselves felt a mixture of these emotions towards their husbands in return.

My suspicion that this is a widespread yet under-reported societal change was again confirmed as I began to write, research and even mention the topic of female breadwinners to friends and colleagues. Their immediate interest demonstrated I was on to something important. So many women would remark excitedly: 'Oh, that's me – or my sister – or all the women in my team.' I was amazed how many women counted as part of this substantial yet largely hidden demographic.

So, what do women who are primary breadwinners look like? What challenges do they face? What are the benefits to their situation? What can we learn from their experiences? Investigating the rise of the female breadwinner is both timely and important in understanding the ever-changing face of the modern *workplace*.

WHY FEMALE BREADWINNERS MATTER

Never before have so many women worked outside the home, nor have our collective wages ever been higher. Certainly, there are many women who are primary breadwinners – single women with or without children and those in lesbian relationships. However, for the purposes of this book, I wanted to focus on women in long-term heterosexual relationships who live with their partners. Because of the way they experience a virtual role-reversal with the men in their lives, these women are re-negotiating gender roles on a daily basis and are bucking social conventions like no other group.

It is vital to investigate this shift because the future of the workforce of tomorrow is increasingly female. Only two of the twelve job titles expected to grow between 2008 and 2018 are dominated by men: accountant and construction worker. In fact, the vast majority of job growth is in fields currently favoured by women, such as teaching, nursing, home health support and customer service.[1] These fields are not as well paid as those previously dominated by men. However, it does indicate that the number of households with a female breadwinner will inevitably increase.

Indeed, the number of women *already* in this category is a large minority. According to 2010 research from the Pew Centre, 22 per cent of American women are now earning more than their husbands. This is a more than fivefold increase from 1970 when it was just four per cent.[2] Similarly, out of all the cohabiting heterosexual couples in Britain where one partner earns more than the other, it was the woman who was the main breadwinner in 25 per cent of the cases by 2007. This is a substantial increase

---

[1] Romano, A & Dokoupil, T 'Men's Lib', *Newsweek* Magazine, September 20, 2010
[2] Fry, R & Cohn, D (2010) 'Women, Men and the New Economics of Marriage', Pew Research Centre

on the five per cent recorded in 1969.[3] Indeed, other surveys of professional women suggest the number is closer to 30 per cent.[4]

We can tell a lot about a couple by the way they interact and how they talk about each other. However, one thing most outsiders can't discern, if both partners work, is which person earns more. Nor might it seem relevant. Yet earnings can underpin how a couple negotiate, how they communicate, their career aspirations, and how they manage family life. The unchallenged assumption, both in the workplace and in social settings, tends to be that men are the main breadwinners.

> *Female breadwinners, though largely invisible, are more common than people anticipate and on the rise.*
>
> •
>
> *They and the men in their lives feel everything from gratitude and support to resentment and competitiveness.*
>
> •
>
> *The fastest growing work sectors are female-dominated.*

THE PERSONAL IS POLITICAL

How might a woman's personal relationships affect her career? We have all heard the adage that *behind every good man is a better woman*. As women begin to succeed in the workplace in greater numbers, and take on greater financial responsibility for their families, are some of them able to draw support from a *better woman* themselves? What if that 'better woman' happens to be a *man?*

---

[3] Doctoral research from Liam Wren-Lewis, PhD student at Oxford University, 2009
[4] Women and Work Survey 2010, *Grazia* Magazine

As an executive coach who specialises in working with women in male-dominated fields, most of my clients are breadwinning wives. During sessions, which focus primarily on work issues, personal relationships will often arise. A woman might be married to a man who works but earns significantly less – or the man might run the household so that *she* can focus on her career to their *joint* benefit.

People often focus on whether successful, professional women in an organisation have children. Children certainly can have a large impact on a woman's career path. However, I was less interested in to whom these women were giving birth, than to whom they were *married*. I know just how vital a supportive spouse is to an individual's career success. I witness it with my clients; I hear it from senior women who are featured in the media; I see it in my own life.

As anyone who has read my first book, *Beyond the Boys' Club: Strategies for Achieving Career Success as a Woman Working in a Male-Dominated Field*, knows, I have a long fascination with how successful women negotiate their career paths. In the book we focus on strategies women use to get ahead in their career such as accessing senior stakeholders, raising their profile, getting credit for their ideas and projecting gravitas when surrounded by male colleagues on a day-to-day basis. While these techniques play a very large part in an individual's success, I have become increasingly certain that who we marry or live with also has a huge impact.

In addition, I had a growing personal interest in the topic. My own husband, Geoff, has historically been the primary breadwinner. However, he is much older than me and will retire in the next decade, just when I expect to be hitting the most productive years of my career. Our financial plans revolve around the expectation that I will then be the primary breadwinner.

Geoff supported me while I finished my PhD around issues facing women in male-dominated fields, and subsequently as I grew my consultancy. I will support him when he wants to slow down. Indeed, he often talks about eventually helping me grow my business further. Like many of the women I talked with, we both recognise that I am the one with the long-term earning potential.

These may be our financial plans, but I have often had niggling questions in the back of my mind. Will things *change* between us when I am the main breadwinner? And if so, how?

These are questions many women face as their career growth outpaces their partner's. Like many other issues in a relationship, the role of the primary breadwinner can be fluid, and changes between partners over time. But one thing is for sure: increasingly, that breadwinner is a woman.

WHERE ARE THE MEN?

While I was able to find a good cross-section of women to speak with, I thought long and hard about how to approach the interviews. In particular, I questioned whether I should interview the men who shared their lives with these women. In my last book, which asked women about their careers, women were happy for their names and even employers' names to be used when discussing their career strategies. However, as I discovered, who brings home the bacon can be a sensitive subject.

For this topic and how it affects relationships, I suspected I would get greater honesty if I made the interviews anonymous and changed all the identifying characteristics. I recognise there are limitations to writing about the lives of women, men and families, as seen exclusively *through the eyes of the women*. However, my intuition was correct.

When I said the interviews would be anonymous, there was almost a collective sigh of relief from tentative women. While some assured me they would be happy for their husbands to be involved, others gave the impression I was getting a truer version of how they felt because there was no danger of their husbands overhearing our conversation or of having to explain to the men in their lives what their answers had been.

At the end of the interviews, some women admitted they had shared more than they'd intended, or that they hadn't realised how complex their feelings were until they started talking about the topic. I must be clear; there was no cloak of secrecy these women held from their partners. Rather, talking to me on their own gave them a freedom to consider their situation as female breadwinners honestly and consciously in a way many had never done before.

Indeed, many said they never gave their primary breadwinner status a thought in their day-to-day lives. Much like the coaching work I do, having a 'safe space' to think about how they *really* felt gave many of them a chance for reflection which they did not frequently give themselves.

My suspicions about the veracity of the answers of couples interviewed together was again confirmed when I read the research of Rebecca Meisenbach, who spent time with female breadwinners. She found that when interviewed *away from their* partners women were more likely to admit they enjoyed the sense of control breadwinning gave them.[5] That being said, ambivalence towards their role was common in her sample, as it was in my own.

Women said they enjoyed the control that earning brought them, but recognised it was a double-edged sword. Other research similarly found that when female breadwinners knew their partners would also be interviewed, they minimised their enjoyment of the role.[6] Reading this research early on had been one of the reasons I opted to interview breadwinner wives but not their male partners.

Similarly, it was not just the truthfulness of the women's statements I wanted to ensure. I did not know how honest most men would be with me. If a man had any seeds of resentment, any lack of confidence regarding his role in the family, would he really want to speak honestly to a female author? Would men I spoke to feel they had to put a gloss on the arrangement? Or would I hear only from men who were very happy in the role?

In fact, while researching this book, a journalist found me who had similarly been looking for 'at-home men' who were willing to admit in the daily papers to neither doing any childcare nor working full-time in any occupation. The silence to her call for volunteers

---

[5] Meisenbach, R (2010) 'The female breadwinner: Phenomenological experience and gendered identity in work/family spaces', *Sex Roles*, 62, 2–19
[6] Stamp, P (1985) 'Balance of financial power in marriage: An exploratory study of breadwinning wives', *Sociological Review*, 33, 546–557

was deafening. When she asked me why she was struggling, I suggested that while I suspect these men exist, they are a minority.

Most men in this position want to be identified for the childcare they provide or the paid work they do in some capacity. Being the unpaid or even lesser-paid partner can carry a real stigma for men. Men who do neither care-giving nor paid work do not seek to trumpet their status to the outside world. As I discovered, there are many men who are described by their wives as completely comfortable with the role – however, there are also some who are not.

In the end, I interviewed 25 women who were primary bread-winners. I was on the hunt for themes and commonalities from which we can learn. Most couples were parents, a few were not. Twenty-two women were married and two were in long-term partnerships. One woman was going through a divorce. Throughout the book I will use the term *husband* and *partner* virtually interchangeably to mean the men with whom these women choose to spend their lives.

NOBODY SETS OUT TO BE A 'GENDER CHAMPION'

You are about to read the stories of women who have experienced the best and worst aspects of being a female breadwinner. We will start by looking at why this issue is increasingly relevant for a rapidly changing workplace. We will identify where the rise of the female breadwinner has come from and its implications for society.

We will then look at how they came to make these arrangements, as their roles were often far from being planned or even static. As one woman, Maggie, a science professor who had been the main breadwinner for more than 20 years, said: 'We never set out to be unconventional!'

We will then look at the feelings and experiences of both the women and the men in these relationships, and finish with the challenges these relationships can pose as well as the tangible benefits to all parties.

It was striking how recognisable these women were. They could be you or me. None would consider themselves a 'superwoman'. They had good days and bad days, both in how they viewed their role as primary breadwinner, and in how they managed being a mother, wife, employee, daughter, colleague and friend.

I am aware that certain stories will seem to suggest that some women have coped with aplomb while others really struggle as primary breadwinners. Yet as I was talking with the women, I was mindful that I was meeting them at a single moment in time. Had I met them three years in the future or three years earlier, I might have got a very different picture.

I would no doubt find that the same woman, who now manages well, struggled in the past. Equally, women who despaired of their relationships in the early days were now back on even ground. The fact that we can relate to and recognise ourselves in these women makes these so stories so inspirational and so useful to learn from.

It would be convenient to think that being a female breadwinner is a static condition and that you either manage or you don't. What I found instead was a real fluidity in their relationships: not just in which partner might be earning more in a given year, but also in how they related to each other and what a couple *needed* from one another as true partners.

I took great comfort in knowing that even if you struggle in the role, the situation can still get much better. Similarly, if everything is smooth sailing now, be mindful of potential problems. Challenges around an income disparity do not automatically doom your relationship or demonstrate that the female breadwinner model is therefore at fault.

The women were reassuringly ordinary in many ways, but there were definite themes that united many of them. I found that while some women who were female breadwinners did indeed have problems in their relationships, it was not the woman's status as higher earner that *caused* the problems. Instead, it was how her role *interacted* with personality characteristics and highlighted the underlying beliefs, expectations and personality characteristics of her or her partner.

I saw questions about what it means to be a modern woman

or man – a good wife, husband and *provider*. I also saw couples grapple with questions around *sense of contribution*. What does it mean to contribute to a household? How do we define our *value* to a relationship? To a family? I did see a sense of greater responsibility, resentment and even hostility.

Equally, I witnessed many positive trends. One was self-confidence. It takes real confidence for men to take up what some might consider a 'secondary' role. And while they are a growing minority, women who out-earn their partners are bucking convention too; as a result, *they* have to be confident. This is vital as they are not only responsible for their family's income, but must also deflect criticism from naysayers regarding their non-traditional choices.

What I saw was very encouraging. These families were creative and pragmatic, playing to their individual talents and personalities, rather than defining themselves according to traditional gender stereotypes that no longer meet the demands and opportunities of modern society. I hope you will enjoy meeting these women as much as I did.

> *20-25 per cent of women who live with their partners are the primary earners in those relationships.*
>
> •
>
> *It takes confidence for both men and women to be in these non-traditional partnerships.*
>
> •
>
> *Choice of partner can affect career as much as the choice of having children.*

1

HOW THE FEMALE BREADWINNER
BENEFITS BUSINESS

*'A woman's place is in the home, which is where she should go
as soon as she gets done at the office.'*
Modern adaptation of the nineteenth-century English proverb

Before we begin to look in depth at the personal lives of the female breadwinners, let's look at how they are becoming the future of the modern workplace. Even with gains for educated women, progress has not been overnight, and equality in accessing senior jobs is still far from secure. Let's start by asking what made the difference in attracting so many women to the workplace.

When we talk about the influx of women into the workforce, we are actually discussing *middle-class* women. Throughout history, out of sheer financial necessity, working-class women have always worked outside the home for pay. This is one reason why feminism has largely been viewed as a movement for middle-class women, despite the benefits it has brought to both genders all across the economic spectrum.

IT'S TOO LATE TO PUT THE GENIE
BACK IN THE BOTTLE

Today, women are in the labour force because they need and want to take advantage of expanded opportunities. Large numbers of middle-class women were first drawn into the workforce in World War II, to take the place of absent men. Once they had tasted the independence that comes from working for pay, many were dissatisfied to return to their 'rightful place' in the home. The genie never quite fitted back in the bottle.

In the 1960s the introduction of the birth control pill, and more crucially its availability for single women, offered women the unprecedented ability to control their fertility. With this came the ability to choose and invest in their education and careers. Women leaving education at this time would have been in no doubt about just how different their lives could be from their mothers' generation. Anti-discrimination legislation in the 1970s made it illegal on both sides of the Atlantic to dismiss a woman for getting married or becoming pregnant.

This opened up higher status jobs: opportunities in male-dominated fields which previously excluded women in any real numbers, such as financial services, information technology, law and the sciences. Higher average educational attainment for women, and the higher prospective wages afforded to these industries, attracted a greater number of women into paid work.[7] Women have never looked back.

OVER-ACHIEVING WOMEN,
UNDER-ACHIEVING MEN

Progress has not been evenly distributed between men and women. As women have capitalised on new career opportunities, men's average *achievement* has simply failed to keep up. Over the past four

---

[7] Blau, F & Kahn, L (2005) 'Changes in the Labor Supply Behavior of Married Women: 1980–2000' Cambridge NBER Working Paper, No. W11230

decades, the number of women in some type of employment steadily increased from 56 per cent in 1971 to 70 per cent in 2008. For men, the complete opposite is happening. During the same period, the number of employed men fell from 92 per cent to 78 per cent.[8]

The current recession has adversely affected the number of men in employment. Manufacturing, construction and financial services initially bore the brunt of lay-offs. Women and the industries where they predominate, such as health and education, until recently have been less affected and as a result women on the whole have suffered fewer redundancies. As the government, education and non-profit sectors are now facing budget cuts, more women will undoubtedly lose out.

Even so, the current recession is only part of the story when it comes to the rise of male unemployment. A decade *before* the recession, in a sample of 4,000 American families during the period 1996-2000, between 13 and 20 per cent of wives out-earned their husbands. This was no temporary fix. In 60 per cent of these families, that pattern of female breadwinning lasted at least three years.[9] Clearly, this demographic is growing but it's not new.

Female breadwinning is most common at either end of the earnings scale. It's noticeable among families where a high-earning woman brings home the majority of the income through a well-paid professional job. However, it's also normal among the working class where both partners are in employment, perhaps with hourly wages, but the woman earns more per hour or works at several jobs simply to make ends meet. In the US, unemployment is certainly higher among all less-educated workers; but a rising share of working-class families is now being headed by female breadwinners.[10]

The reality of women as primary breadwinners is here – but it is far from being an overnight sensation. This has been a gradual change which we have largely ignored. In the US, men's share of the total labour force has declined from 70 per cent in 1945 to less

---

[8] Office for National Statistics (2009) 'Women in the Labour Market'
[9] Winkler, A, McBride, T, Andrews, C (2005) 'Women who out-earn their husbands: A transitory or persistent phenomenon for couples?', *Demography*, 42 (3), August, 523–535
[10] US Bureau of Labor Statistics, June 2010

than 50 per cent in 2010. There is an increasing need for men to redefine masculinity according to what works *now*.

Andrew Romano and Tony Dokoupil explained in a cover article, aptly titled 'Men's Lib' for *Newsweek* magazine: '...There are good reasons why inner-city fathers, hedge fund honchos and former GM plant managers aren't taking several months off from work to care for their kids – or exploring new fields, like nursing, where few of today's men dare to tread. Most guys, in fact, don't even need rescuing – *or at least not yet*. They're still overrepresented in business and government, earn more on the dollar... and clean fewer dishes.'[11]

Getting men on board is easier said than done, even though a rapidly changing future is staring them in the face.

BEHIND EVERY GREAT WOMAN...

Coinciding with these new opportunities for women, the appeal of the supportive male partner or husband has never been greater. Certainly, many of the female breadwinners I spoke with were effusive in the credit they gave their partners in being supportive of their careers. These men served as mentors, cheerleaders, offered career 'reality checks' and a shoulder to cry on in addition to the day-to-day support in running a household and family.

Increasingly, I think it is this personal relationship which is the most important to a woman's success. If you struggle at home, it is harder to focus on the job. If you feel guilty about what you are not doing for your family, you will not be able to concentrate. If you fear your partner's resentment, you cannot enjoy your successes.

In fact, many of the most successful women in the world have taken advantage of changing social attitudes and married men who are happy to be supportive husbands. Indra Nooyi, CEO of Pepsi and one of the world's most powerful businesswomen, is married to a man who quit his job and became a consultant to fit in with his wife and children. The same thing happened for

---

[11] Romano, A & Dokoupil, T 'Men's Lib', *Newsweek* Magazine, September 20, 2010

Kraft CEO, Irene Rosenfeld, whose husband decided to become a self-employed financial consultant 20 years ago to help her career. The husband of Angela Ahrendts, the CEO of Burberry, left his construction business so that Angela could move to London to take up her post.

In my own life, my husband serves as my greatest mentor and biggest source of support. We have at various times worked together in the same organisation. As frequently as I consult him on a work issue, he will also say how much he has learned from me. We take almost daily walks which serve as career boosts. They are an opportunity to share the challenges of the day, brainstorm options and share our professional and family goals.

I believe men like my husband are the future. This is an exciting time for the modern man and woman; we can determine how to flourish in our chosen roles, irrespective of our gender.

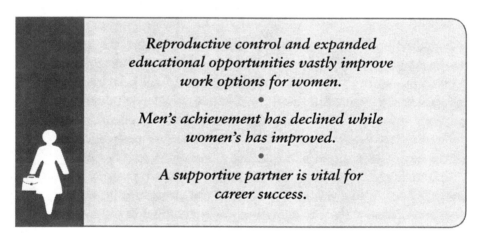

Reproductive control and expanded educational opportunities vastly improve work options for women.

•

Men's achievement has declined while women's has improved.

•

A supportive partner is vital for career success.

ENOUGH 'FIXING' THE WOMEN

An increasing number of organisations recognise that ignoring gender as a key issue and hoping women will just 'trickle up the pipeline' is not working. Over the past several decades employers have attempted to attract and develop women through internal women's networks and career development training. I do believe these initiatives have their place and have already helped many women rise in their careers. They offer supportive environments and provide women with the tools to 'play the game' according to the rules of a male-designed workplace.

However, these programmes are often premised on the idea of women 'fixing themselves'. Approaching deeply ingrained cultural issues with underfunded networks run by well-intentioned but time-pressed volunteers has its clear limitations. Gender must be seen as a business issue.

However, not all organisations can see the curve ahead. A survey by McKinsey found that only 28 per cent of companies have gender diversity as an item on their top ten strategic agenda, while 40 per cent don't have it on their agenda at all.[12] This issue is not even on the radar of many organisations. However, those who can see how the workforce is changing can reap the benefits of a diverse leadership team if they make gender balance a business issue *now*.

Companies need to value the *differences* between men and women. Allowing women to use influence on their own terms is vital to reap the benefits they can add. They must be lauded, rather than chastised for their different perspectives and priorities. A survey by McKinsey found that leaders agreed that the leadership behaviours that will be of particular importance over the next five years are also the behaviours in which women are deemed to be stronger: intellectual stimulation, inspiration, participative decision-making and the setting of clear expectations and rewards.[13]

Women are more likely to accept part-time and temporary contracts, and because of the pay gap are often cheaper to employ and valuable because of their different strengths. As explained by Madeleine Bunting in her book *Willing Slaves*, the overwork culture has crippled the equal opportunities revolution for men and women: 'Employers over the last 20 years haven't done women any favours by employing them [women]; they wanted the labour for many reasons ranging from the fact that it was cheap, to the fact that many of the emotional skills women have

---

[12] McKinsey & Co (2010) 'Women Leaders, a Competitive Edge After the Crisis'
[13] McKinsey & Co (2008) 'Women Matter 2: Female Leadership as a Competitive Edge for the Future'

honed for generations are in demand in running organisations.'[14]

Organisations that fail to capitalise on the *strengths* of women, and rather hope they will become more like men, are missing a trick. Indeed there is even evidence that investors are beginning to see gender equality as a strategic business and investment issue.[15]

THE CASE FOR FEMALE BREADWINNERS: EDUCATING THE BOARD OF TOMORROW

The business case for moving towards gender balance, a balance that will enable even more women to take on primary breadwinning roles, is based on three main facts we will explore.

I recently helped judge a contest for MBA students at one of the top universities in the UK. The students had to work in teams and explain to the judges how they had turned around a hypothetical failing product line, using clever marketing and a new sales strategy. I was the only female judge at the competition, and voted equally with the other eight older, white, male judges as to which team deserved the prize.

The three highest-scoring teams were comprised solely of women. In fact, the overall winning team was made up of five Chinese women. One of the judges said to the audience when looking at their smiling faces: 'You're looking at the future and where we're headed.' Honestly, I can't be sure whether he was referring to the fact that the team was made up of women or that they were Chinese. But in either case, he's right.

Women across the world are entering education in unprecedented numbers in both Europe and North America but also in the new power-house economies such as India, China and Russia. They are following an example of expansion of educational and job opportunities that was set several decades earlier in the West.

In the lecturing I do to university students, I see an emerging

---

[14] Bunting, M (2004) *Willing Slaves: How the Overwork Culture is Ruling our Lives*, HarperCollins
[15] Calvert, P (2010) 'Investors Put Gender on the Agenda', World and Walden Asset Management

confidence among young women, and with good reason. Over lunch a few months ago, I was discussing with another academic their recent round of scholarship applications. For his department, 21 of the 24 new scholarships were being awarded to women.

He admitted: 'We were not doing it for the sake of affirmative action or to help bolster our numbers of women. The young female candidates we saw were just so much more impressive than the men. The girls spoke eloquently and had usually handled a range of extracurricular and charitable activities, in addition to getting good grades by the time they got to university. We just didn't see the same calibre of boys this year.'

After the expansion of UK higher education in the 1980s, few analysts expected women to exceed men in participation. The initial predictions had been that social mobility would be most prevalent across *social class*, not gender. Perhaps surprisingly to the original legislators, it was the engagement of *women* with higher education which has seen the most progress.

By 2007–2008, the participation rate of women aged 18–30 was 49 per cent, compared with 38 per cent for men of a similar age. Women don't wait until university to catch up, either; girls now outperform boys at all key stages.[16] Across the world, women are entering university in droves. By 2016, it is estimated that women will earn 60 per cent of all Bachelors, 63 per cent of all Masters and 54 per cent of all Doctorate and professional degrees in the US.[17]

The projections are no different in other developed countries. By 2015, women in Poland, Italy, Australia, Hungary, Germany and France will account for over 60 per cent of university graduates. More amazingly, women in Sweden and the UK are predicted to make up over 70 per cent of all university graduates by 2015.[18]

No wonder the under-achievement of school-age *boys* is an increasingly hot topic among educators.

---

[16] UK Higher Education Policy Unit (2009) 'Male and Female Participation and Progression in Higher Education'

[17] US Department of Education, National Center for Education Statistics, Projections of Education Statistics to 2016, Higher Education General Information Survey

[18] Organisation for Economic Cooperation and Development (OECD) (2008) 'The Reversal of Gender Inequalities: An Ongoing Trend in Higher Education to 2030' Volume 1 – Demography

COURTING FEMALE CONSUMERS

Women are increasingly being recognised as a market of choice. We are now past the age of the 'pink phone' or a conveniently placed lipstick-holder in a new car as manufacturers' nods to attracting female consumers. Globally, women control $20 trillion in consumer spending annually. That figure is estimated to grow by as much as 40 per cent in the next five years alone.

In the US, women influence $4.3 trillion of the $5.9 trillion in all consumer spending; this means that 73 per cent of all consumer purchases are influenced by women.[19] The story is similar in the UK, where women are responsible for 70 per cent of all household purchasing decisions and hold almost half of the UK's wealth.[20] These are dramatic figures, yet women have historically been mis-understood by marketers.

As explained in the book on marketing to women, *Women Want More*: 'A quiet economic and social revolution is taking place... It is a revolution of dissatisfaction in which women are using their checkbooks to vote no on large sectors of the economy, including financial services, consumer electronics, consumer durables and healthcare... The bad news is that only a small percentage of companies understand the significance of the female economy to their business. If they respond to this economy at all, they do so by fiddling with segmentation or by making small adjustments to their product line or to their organisations, as if these powerful trends were nothing more than incremental shifts in existing patterns.

'The good news is that some companies do recognise the opportunity and respond to it brilliantly, with skill, nuance, and genuine engagement. They enjoy breakout growth, unprecedented consumer loyalty and category dominance.'[21]

Strategic organisations, particularly those in consumer-facing industries, are recognising the need to address the value and needs

---

[19] Silverstein, MJ & Sayre, K (2009) 'The Female Economy', *Harvard Business Review*
[20] Diversity and Gender Balance in Britain: A Study by TCAM in conjunction with *The Observer* as part of the *Good Companies Guide* (2009) London
[21] Silverstein, M & Sayre, K (2009) *Women Want More: How to Capture Your Share of the World's Largest, Fastest-Growing Market* HarperCollins

of the modern woman. Leaders developing and selling goods and services for this market must reflect these changes. In retrospect, it now seems naïve of us *ever* to have thought a leadership team made up of one type of consumer – predominantly older, white, men – could adequately design and offer services to such a diverse global marketplace.

WOMEN AND THE BOTTOM LINE

The Lord Davies report, *Women on Boards,* published in the UK in 2011, highlighted the increasingly recognised fact that it makes financial sense to have women sitting on boards of directors.[22] Research indicated that companies with more women on their boards outperform their rivals with a 42 per cent higher return in sales, 66 per cent higher return on invested capital and 53 per cent higher return on equity.[23]

Female directors enhance board independence and encourage better decision-making.[24] How does this happen? The complementary skills of a gender-diverse board foster creativity, limit 'group think' and anticipate potential blind spots.[25]

Women on boards also appear to pay attention to the seemingly simple things that make a big difference. For example, research suggests women are more likely to take their non-executive director roles more seriously, preparing notes and doing the reading ahead of meetings. They are more likely to ask tough questions and to challenge decisions which others might think just need to be nodded through.[26]

Undoubtedly, this is a real strength in a post-recession world. Indeed, my husband, who has held a range of senior jobs over

[22] Lord Davies (2011) 'Women on Boards' Department for Business Innovation and Skills
[23] Joy, L et al (2007) 'The Bottom Line: Corporate Performance and Women's Representation on Boards', *Catalyst,* New York
[24] Fondas, N & Sassolos, S (2000) 'A Different Voice in the Boardroom: How the Presence of Women Directors Affects Board Influence over Management', *Global Focus,* 12, 13–22
[25] Frose, M & Szebel-Habig, A (2009) *Mixed Leadership,* Haupt Verlag
[26] Burke, R & Mattis, M (Eds) (2000) 'Women on Corporate Boards of Directors: International Challenges and Opportunities', 75–6

the fourteen years I have known him, has often remarked that in interviews and in reporting to boards, it is normally the few women who ask the toughest questions.

A Canadian study found that boards from a range of non-profit, private and public sector organisations benefited from better governance if they had *at least three* women. The 30 per cent mark appears to be the tipping point for the widest benefits. This is the point at which individual female board members cease to be seen as representatives of their entire gender and are taken seriously as individuals.

The more gender-balanced boards were more likely to identify criteria for measuring strategy and monitoring its implementation. They were also more likely to adhere to a code of conduct. They gave more attention to non-financial performance measures such as employee and customer satisfaction, diversity and corporate social responsibility.[27]

The ethics of business are vital to women. I have met dozens of women who leave organisations because they feel their sense of ethics and integrity is increasingly at odds with that of their employers.

To this point, jokes abound about how the lack of women in senior leadership positions may have contributed to the recent recession. We ask: 'Would the damage have been as great if it had been Lehman Sisters, instead of Lehman Brothers?' While the question may have started in jest, there is good evidence that women on boards may contribute to solvency, a key concern in today's recovering economy. A study by Leeds Business School found that having at least one female director on the board appears to cut a company's chances of going bust by 20 per cent, and that having two or three female directors lowered the chances of bankruptcy even further.[28]

Forward-thinking organisations recognise that better corporate governance led by better gender representations add quickly to profits. The evidence has been mounting over the last decade and the

---

[27] Brown, D et al (2002) 'Women on Boards: Not Just the Right Thing…But the Bright Thing', Conference Board of Canada

[28] Professor Nick Wilson LUBS 'Women in the Boardroom Help Companies Succeed' *The Times*, March 19, 2009

results should be hard for any proactive business leader to ignore. Women in senior management make bottom-line sense.

Women are outpacing men in education.

•

Women make at least 70 per cent of all consumer decisions.

•

Women in senior management deliver better profitability.

QUESTION THE PRACTICE OF 'EQUAL OPPORTUNITIES'

What can proactive organisations that want to attract and develop good women actually do? Culture change and a redefining of success are required.

Women are offered *equal opportunities* to climb the ladder to career success. However, this definition of 'equality' is stacked against women right from the start, given the traditional expectation that they will handle full-time responsibilities both at home and at work. Working women have done all the accommodating in terms of time, energy and personal sacrifice without reaching true workplace integration.

Women have been offered the *right to equality* in a system that can't possibly work for them. Certainly, many female breadwinners do have help at home from their partners, but I was amazed how many women I met still shoulder the lion's share of the home-life responsibilities, despite having a partner who could handle a greater share of the household duties. What working woman has not half-jokingly lamented: 'I need a wife!'

In the first case, organisations must stop using the traditional male model of work. This is an outmoded concept of a career without breaks, a willingness for international travel and the ability to network after hours, all seen as ways to demonstrate commitment. This model is based on the increasingly outmoded expectation that someone is at home full-time to keep the paid worker and family supplied with meals, clean clothes and the other mechanics of a well-oiled home life.

As we will see, this is not a model that works for most female breadwinners. The women I met did not want to spend more time at work regardless of their breadwinning status. Additionally, this model is increasingly at odds with modern *men*, particularly those married to female breadwinners or those who want to prioritise family life in a way their own fathers did not.

LET GO OF THE GLAMOUR OF 'EXTREME JOBS'

More women than ever before, particularly those who are prime breadwinners, are taking on 'extreme jobs'. These types of jobs are particularly unappealing to women, but are increasingly seen as necessary just to maintain a professional standing. This type of role can appear glamorous initially but is unsustainable for men or women, no matter who is the main earner.

Adam Quinton, a faculty member of the Gender and Policy Program at the School of International and Public Affairs at Columbia University says: 'Because the hours for so many high level jobs are demanding for any person, male or female, you get far fewer women. Wrongly or rightly, women shoulder more family responsibilities. A relationship can be hard enough. Having two individuals going at 100 miles per hour means their relationship can derail. The support has to be there to enable the primary breadwinner to manage such extreme jobs.'

Many of my coaching clients are married to equally ambitious men, and it can cause real problems as family demands increase. Couples often pair up as peers, often at university, business school or in first jobs. There will be an unspoken assumption that after children arrive, it will be the woman's career that will take the back seat.

Interestingly, it is often the couples who work in *different* sectors, or where it is understood that one person is more ambitious than the other, that have the most straightforward discussions around career plans. They are rarely competing or resentful of the other's success because direct comparisons are difficult to make.

When asked how business should be addressing the growing number of female breadwinners, Adam answers: 'There is a double-whammy on its way, as we are graduating more women from university and postgraduate programmes, plus we are retiring a huge number of baby-boomer men. Organisations are just not set up to deal with this. They are realising the majority of middle managers are women, and the people coming up after them are certainly women who want to work differently.

'Organisations can't continue to get by hiring ad hoc maternity cover and hoping for the best. There has to be a more strategic way of attracting women back, otherwise they are facing a huge hole in their pipeline of talent. If they don't do it, it shows junior women the company won't develop them and offer them non-linear careers. Instead, women will leave for a competitor who will.'

Do five or more of these apply to your role? Then you're in an extreme job

Unpredictable flow of work

•

Large amount of travel

•

Tight deadlines and a fast pace

•

After-hours work events

•

24/7 availability to clients

•

Responsibility for profit and loss

•

Mentoring and recruiting

•

Expectation of physical presence at the office at least ten hours a day

SOME MOTHERS DO 'AVE 'EM – FLEXIBLE WORKING

Treating flexible working as a right for *all* employees is another step in the right direction. Too frequently, flexible working is seen as a *working mothers'* issue. This is despite the fact that many fathers would like to work more flexibly, as indeed would people who are not parents. Maintaining 'balance' as an issue only for working mothers marginalises them as being 'demanding' or 'difficult' and stigmatises the issue of flexible working as a whole.

Even in organisations that do have family-friendly policies, women are often reluctant to take advantage of them, either because they fear being judged as less committed or because too frequently access relies on management discretion.[29] While it may be hard enough for women to ask for part-time work, it is doubly hard for men to ask for fear of being seen as less ambitious or committed. It is vital to open up the opportunities for flexible working to everyone, as a good proportion of men are partnered with women who are high earners; these men need and deserve flexible schemes as well.

Similarly, to get the best out of their people, male or female, organisations must measure performance on *results* rather than *hours*. As you will see, one thing was clear: being the main breadwinner did not mean that women wanted to spend more hours at the office. They prided themselves on doing a good job in a shorter period of time.

We've all witnessed the trick of leaving a coat on the back of your chair to suggest you were working late or sending out after-hours emails to remind colleagues you are still hard at work. However, most women I work with find these ruses disingenuous and would rather be judged on their merits, without having to play the long-hours game. Quite understandably, they do not want to be unfavourably compared with others who could put in more 'face-time' at the office while offering merely the same or poorer results.

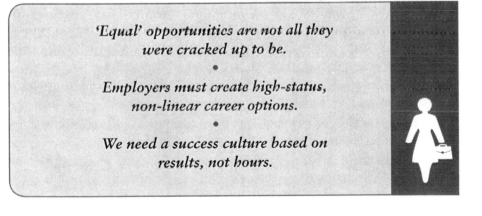

> *'Equal' opportunities are not all they were cracked up to be.*
>
> •
>
> *Employers must create high-status, non-linear career options.*
>
> •
>
> **We need a success culture based on results, not hours.**

[29] Lewis, S & Taylor, K (1996) 'Evaluating the Impact of Family-Friendly Employer Policies' from Lewis, S *The Work-Family Challenge: Rethinking Employment*, London, Thousand Oaks and New Delhi, Sage

ABOLISH AGE LIMITS FOR SPOTTING 'HIGH POTENTIAL'

Employers must recognise that people's work priorities change at different life stages. When certain employees feel ready to wind down is exactly the time when others will be looking for fresh mental stimulation. The traditional trajectory focused on a man's career being most active in his twenties and thirties, with a slow tailing-off as he entered his fifties. This is the model to which all employees are expected to adhere. Women, on the other hand, have their prime childbearing years during their twenties and thirties and their careers often peak a full decade later than those of their male peers.[30]

The real problem comes from the unofficial age limits imposed for spotting those deemed 'high potential'. These programmes, which aim to fast-track certain individuals with promise, miss a good deal of talent. They seek to identify those employees worthy of extra development and training, in their twenties and thirties – again, the worst time for many women.

I meet women every day whose children are now in school or who have left home who say: 'I'm now ready to get back to full-time work. I crave more of a mental challenge and have the energy to take on more responsibility.' Yet these same women, tarred with the unfavourable brush of *working mother* are often viewed as the least promising and interesting of potential applicants. What if companies could regard women career-returners, or those in their late forties and fifties whose children are older or have left home, as having the same superstar potential as younger employees? Who knows what those women could achieve in what could be the most productive years of their careers?

Forward-thinking organisations use alumni programmes to keep in touch with previous employees who may have left for a variety of reasons. Perhaps they left to raise children, or maybe they went to work for a competitor or even started freelance

---

[30] Schaffnit-Chatterjee (2009) 'Who is Washing the Dishes Tonight? The Gender Gap in Household Work', Deutsche Bank Research, March 2009

work that fitted in with their schedules better. Smart employers encourage people who have perhaps scaled back their hours, when children or eldercare duties demanded it, to consider new opportunities as their caring responsibilities ease over time.

Caring responsibilities change as time goes on and these past employees could become prime candidates to develop when they are ready to take on more professional challenges later. Organisations which want to develop their diverse talent pool can no longer afford to smugly assume they can determine an employee's potential by the time that person is 30 years old.

WILL SHE OR WON'T SHE? HOW GENDERED ASSUMPTIONS LIMIT POTENTIAL

For too long, assumptions about what women can or cannot do have limited their progress. Most women, whether they are the primary breadwinner or not, speak of real annoyance at the assumptions about their limitations. Some felt overlooked when new opportunities or promotions were announced, as a result of employers' assumptions about their capabilities or goals after they'd had children; as if they were now automatically less ambitious.

Ironically, even single women were not immune to the gendered assumptions of colleagues. These affected women before they'd even had children, as impending marriages would often spark debate as to how long it would be until they began to have children, and hence became less committed. Women who returned from maternity leave spoke of others' prying questions as to when they would be having more children.

Similarly, I met breadwinning women who were mothers and keen to take on international placements. They recognised the opportunity as a career progression, and in many cases as a way of teaching their children about other cultures. Of course, these women bristled at being overlooked for these types of roles on the assumption they would not want them simply because they were working mothers.

International placements are another key aspect of organisational expectations that can be unhelpful to female breadwinners and the men who support them. For sure, the increase in the number of female breadwinners with supportive partners at home means these types of roles are now viable for some. Just as employers should not assume that women eschew international travel, they cannot assume that men want these roles either. Increasingly, they are married to women who are the main earners, and so considering such overseas contracts is just as difficult for them as it has been historically for women.

The key is in having the dialogue with employers and not assuming that these types of placements will or won't work primarily based on a person's gender.

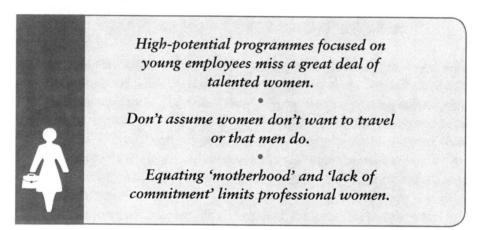

> *High-potential programmes focused on young employees miss a great deal of talented women.*
>
> •
>
> *Don't assume women don't want to travel or that men do.*
>
> •
>
> *Equating 'motherhood' and 'lack of commitment' limits professional women.*

'QUIET' LEADERSHIP: NOT REWARDING SHE WHO SHOUTS LOUDEST

We must rethink our assumptions about what makes someone ready to take on a leadership position. Historically, we have operated on a model that rewarded those who shouted loudest, something I myself have encouraged women to do more. Quite plainly, with the traditional masculine model of work, actively asking for such opportunities was the surest way to be considered. However, more consideration must be given to those who are not necessarily putting hands up for their roles. These people, more often than not, are women.

I meet countless women who flourish in leadership positions they initially doubted they could master. They are not self-promoters by nature and their advancement into that leadership role often came from *someone else* recognising the wisdom in her different approach to leadership. That person, usually a well-meaning mentor, saw them as perfect for the role; and with coaching and support, the women succeeded.

This type of leader is humbled by their sense of responsibility for others. They recognise that a good leader *serves* their team, not the other way around. There is reciprocal loyalty in these teams. They are humble stewards, and I believe that in the modern workforce, we need more humility than ever for these types of people-managing roles.

To this end, senior management should look to promote not necessarily those who *say* they would be good leaders, but those who are already *acting* as good leaders. This should not be the challenge it might initially sound, as we all know managers who do not inspire confidence and trust. Look for people of whom colleagues speak well, employees to whom others turn when they have a question, those who are able to engage and inspire the widest range of people.

Leadership style and language also has to become more inclusive, and respectful of a variety of perspectives. Too frequently we think of women as having cornered the market on collaboration and consensus-building and men as always being very direct and to the point.

The truth, as anyone who has ever worked with a variety of people knows, is that these generalisations can help us understand trends but are in no way adequate in predicting our experiences. Smart organisations are waking up to the fact that those leaders who can 'flex' a collaborative and directive style depending on the situation are those who will inspire the most people and get the best out of their teams.

I worked with one European multinational company which had with an unspoken rule that career ambition was demonstrated by taking on a new international assignment every two years. The women I coached, most of whom were main breadwinners, felt that this type of constant upheaval was too much to ask of their husbands and children. Needless to say, this expectation placed a huge strain on both them and their partners. It also meant most women at the company questioned whether they wanted even to attempt to progress to the next level with this organisation.

As one of my clients at the company, a female breadwinner deemed *high potential,* eloquently said: 'I look ahead of me, and all the leaders of this company are divorced, live in separate countries from their families or are willing to continually uproot them across the globe just so they can work every weekend. Are those qualities the ones we even want to reward with leadership? If so, it's not for me.'

This begs the question: how wise is it to have companies headed by people who are willing to sacrifice every aspect of their personal lives? What implicit message is being sent about the types of people we reward with senior positions? Is it any wonder more women don't want to emulate this definition of *success*?

Instead it may be wiser in the long term to question the long-held assumption that those who visibly want power are in the best position to exercise it. As explained in *Why Women Mean Business* by Aviva Wittenberg-Cox and Allison Maitland: 'Perhaps those best able to exercise the responsibility and service of leadership are those not particularly hungering after power.'[31]

MIND THE *PAY* GAP

To what do female breadwinners attribute their success? In a 2010 US *Redbook* magazine survey, breadwinning wives did not feel particularly strategic about their careers, nor that they worked longer hours than their partners. Instead, they recognised that they were more highly educated and so landed more *lucrative* jobs.[32]

---

[31] Wittenberg-Cox, A & Maitland, A (2009) *Why Women Mean Business*, Wiley
[32] Goad, K (2010) 'Big earning wives, and the men who love them', *MSN Lifestyle*, September 13

As we have seen, women are capitalising on unprecedented educational opportunities. Quite rightly, this wave of educated women expects to be paid at a level commensurate with their skills. Women's earnings grew 44 per cent between 1970 and 2007, compared with a mere six per cent growth for men. This sharper growth has enabled women to narrow, but not close, the earnings gap with men.

To this end, median earnings of full-year female workers in 2007 were 71 per cent of the earnings of comparable men. This was a rise from a paltry 52 per cent in 1970.[33]

In the past, employers often viewed working women as being the secondary provider to a male breadwinner. This effectively legitimised paying women less. It contributed to the concept of the 'family wage': a salary for one person that could support an entire family. The concept of the family wage has been all but eradicated, yet the gender pay gap has remained.

Naila Kabeer of the University of Sussex explained in an article for *Open Democracy* why women are fast becoming the preferred global labour source for many employers. It's because of the pay gap: 'Women have emerged as the flexible labour force par excellence. Women workers are less likely to be organised [in unions] than men, they can be paid less on the grounds of their purported secondary earner status, and they have less bargaining power because of the limitations placed on their labour market options by unpaid domestic responsibilities.'[34]

Clearly, part of the appeal of women for employers globally is their perceived ability to be 'managed' more easily because of their limited negotiating power.

Pay equality is one way in which organisations demonstrate their commitment to attracting and retaining talented women. Much progress has been made in recent years at encouraging parity. However, in fields with discretionary pay elements such as

---

[33] Fry, R & Cohn, D (2010) 'Women, Men and the New Economics of Marriage', Pew Research Centre
[34] Kabeer, N (2008) 'Marriage, Motherhood and Masculinity in the Global Economy', University of Sussex, January 29, www.opendemocracy.net

financial services, women earn up to 47 per cent less than men.[35]

Bonuses are often too subjective and left to managerial discretion which is subject to unconscious bias at best. There is a problematic lack of transparency. Indeed, organisations will go to lengths to protect that lack of clarity, such as termination of those who seek to compare salaries with colleagues. This all suggests that until employees have far greater transparency in how discretionary pay is awarded and how they compare with colleagues, there can be little progress in pay equality.

The pay differential cannot be explained solely by women leaving to have children either, as most women in these positions start on lower initial salaries as well. This means women, particularly if they are responsible for all of a family's income, are doubly losing out – first by the likelihood of being underpaid merely because of their gender, and secondly by not having a financially contributing man to bolster the family income.

Organisations need to rectify pay inequities for several reasons. Women are increasingly *choosing* organisations with a commitment to equality, in deed and not just in word. The establishment of lists in the UK that publicise 'Top 100 Employers for Women' or 'Where Women Want to Work' are evidence of the greater awareness that talented women have more choice than generations of women before.

At a time when more women are taking up the mantle of primary breadwinner, a gendered pay gap can no longer be tolerated. It's just not good for any employer who wants to attract the best talent. Any discrepancies will encourage this group of hard-working women to take their skills to an employer who will pay them at a rate commensurate with their skills, and that number of women is rapidly growing.

---

[35] Equality and Human Rights Commission (2009) 'eFinance Sector Inquiry', September 7, 2009

WALK THE WALK, NOT JUST TALK
THE DIVERSITY TALK

How can employers get the best out of this rising tide of female breadwinners? Adam Quinton of Columbia University says: 'Employers need to *act* on their policies. You can have great written policies, but it's easy to get a feel for how much a company actually *practises* equality. Anyone can have a statement of intent, but companies need to do the much harder work of changing the culture.

'Ultimately, it means stopping the decision-making loop where all the decisions are made at the highest levels by white men, far too many of whom currently don't see this as a huge issue because they don't think it affects them. Organisations are unsustainable if they don't take it seriously.'

Adam explains the reticence some leaders have towards taking decisive action around equality: 'It's like the budget deficit: people see it as a big problem in the future, but it's not going to cripple an organisation tomorrow. So it's easier to do nothing, and hope that the next CEO takes care of it.

'Additionally, you become an easy target if you try to institute change that doesn't bear fruit immediately or, God forbid, there are any other problems. For example, some heavy hitters in the US were coming around to the idea that women were the future of leadership right before the recession. In the backlash some critics complained CEOs had become distracted by 'women's issues' and taken their eye off the ball.

'You can understand why leaders don't want to be seen to take such huge risks around diversity. It requires a long-term vision and a departure from the norm.'

To reap the rewards of the widest possible talent pool requires employers to create an inclusive atmosphere for women. The model of 'fixing the women' to be more like the men is no longer viable. At best it patronises the same women organisations want to keep and reinforces the idea that gender diversity is a 'women's issue' alone.

At worst, it seeks to perpetuate a single cultural mindset that clearly will not work for organisations in the long run. Why should we teach women to ignore their own strengths to take on the worst qualities of men? Wouldn't we get further by helping both men and women take on the best of both perspectives? It is time to redesign organisational culture and values.

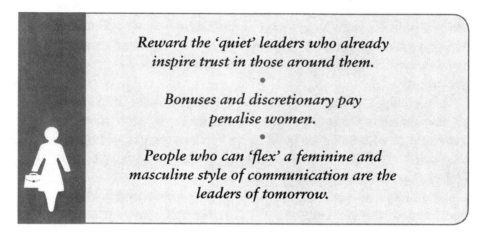

Reward the 'quiet' leaders who already inspire trust in those around them.

•

Bonuses and discretionary pay penalise women.

•

People who can 'flex' a feminine and masculine style of communication are the leaders of tomorrow.

2

WHY THE FEMALE BREADWINNER
BENEFITS MEN

'At present, we insist that a woman be treated just the same as a man. Are we sure we want to be treated as most men are in our society? Or do both sexes deserve something better?'

KAY KEESHAN HAMOD
Working It Out

So, why is the rise of the female breadwinner important – and can this shift benefit men too?

According to 2010 research from the Pew Centre, 22 per cent of American women are now earning more than their husbands. This is a more than fivefold increase from 1970 when it was just four per cent.[36] Similarly, out of all the cohabiting heterosexual couples in Britain where one half earns more than the other, it was the woman who was the main breadwinner in 25 per cent of the cases by 2007. This is a substantial increase on the five per cent recorded in 1969.[37]

Indeed, other surveys of professional women suggest the number is closer to 30 per cent.[38] Women were once defined as the *emotional* provider and men the *economic* provider, though that is slowly changing. Now more women than ever are taking on the

---

[36] Fry, R & Cohn, D (2010) 'Women, Men and the New Economics of Marriage', Pew Research Centre

[37] Doctoral research from Liam Wren-Lewis, PhD student at Oxford University, 2009

[38] Women and Work Survey 2010, *Grazia* Magazine

label *economic provider* as well. Women in these roles can feel a mix of gratitude, confusion, resentment, uncertainty, hostility, anger or even denial.

More American men are married to women whose education and income exceed their own, compared to their counterparts in the 1970s,[39] and the prevalence of this trend varies internationally. In Germany, it is relatively uncommon, whereas in the US it is larger and growing.[40]

From an economic perspective, these trends have contributed to a gender role reversal in the gains from marriage. In the past, when relatively few middle-class wives worked, marriage enhanced the economic status of women more than that of men. In recent decades, however, the economic gains associated with marriage have been *greater* for men than for women.

DR JONES, DO YOU TAKE THIS MAN TO BE YOUR WEDDED HUSBAND?

Part of the reason for the superior gains of married adults is compositional in nature. Since 1970, marriage rates have declined, the most sharply for the least educated men and women. Highly educated people, however, are still getting married, and husbands are reaping the financial rewards. Forty years ago, the typical man did not gain another breadwinner in his household when he married. Today, he does.

This gives his household increased earning power that most unmarried men do not enjoy. Marrying educated working women has enabled men to enjoy an easier economic life than ever before. Indeed, on our travels together, my husband and I have checked into plenty of hotels at which they address him as Dr Doyle-Morris, assuming he is the one with the professional title. As my

---

[39] Fry, R & Cohn, D (2010) 'Women, Men and the New Economics of Marriage', Pew Research Centre

[40] Blossfeld, HP & Timm, A (Eds) (2003) *Who Marries Whom? Educational Systems as Marriage Markets in Modern Societies*, Dordrecht, Netherlands: Kluwer Academic Publishers

own husband jokes as he passes me the room reservation in front of the hotel staff, this is a great time to be a man married to an educated woman.

Indeed, as the number of women earning degrees has increased and the pay gap between men and women in full-time employment has shrunk somewhat, highly educated women are still marrying, and increasingly to men with less education. In fact, the household earnings of single men have dropped 16 per cent since the 1970s.

This is in stark contrast to single women, married women and married men, all of whom have enjoyed average household earnings' gains of 60 per cent during the same period – all due to the increased financial contributions of working women. This is fantastic news for married men. They are enjoying increased household income with decreasing pressure to be the person who solely provides it.[41]

THE INVISIBLE SUPERWOMAN:
NOW YOU SEE HER, NOW YOU DON'T

While myths abound about the female breadwinner, the truth is you wouldn't know one if she stared you in the face. She is you; she is me; she is the woman next to you. Unless she discusses what she and her husband do to earn a living, it is unlikely you would ever know she earns more than her partner. Many downplay their status and the reliance the family have on her income.

And why shouldn't she? Rarely is the press or public opinion favourable towards stereotypes about women who 'bring home the bacon'.

There is too frequently an assumption reminiscent of the 1950s, that wives who out-earn their husbands risk 'emasculating' their partners, rendering them powerless and disregarding their self-esteem. They throw their weight around at home and generally 'wear the trousers'.

---

[41] Current Population Survey: Version 2.0 Minneapolis, Minnesota Population Centre (producer & distributor) 2009

That image couldn't be further from the truth. In fact, most women take pains to tell their partners how grateful they are and indeed make sure they also share the domestic chores with their partners.

What type of woman would marry a man knowing the burden of breadwinning would always primarily be hers? What could possibly be the benefits to her? Certainly, some did not anticipate the role; they became primary breadwinners due to a partner's illness, disability or unemployment. But contrary to what you might expect, many women were primary breadwinners by their family's choice.

For the purposes of this book, I focused on the experiences of women who had been the main breadwinners for at least three years. Demographically, women ranged in age from early thirties to recently retired women in their sixties. They were of different ethnicities and cultural backgrounds. The women interviewed were primarily British, with several American and continental European women taking part as well.

Some women I interviewed earned just over half the family income. Others brought home 100 per cent of the money. Some had husbands who worked full-time and others were married to men who ran the household to help facilitate *her* success. As with all couples, some seemed happier than others with their situations.

Some of my findings echoed an Australian study which found that the majority of breadwinning women (70 per cent) they interviewed were in the situation due to economic necessity rather than a commitment to equality. The Australian husbands in this 'necessity' category had less education and less experience in professional and managerial roles. Additionally, these men were not committed to gender role reversal and were less involved in either housework or childcare. They may well have wished for a return to the traditional male breadwinner role, but the changing face of the labour structure meant this was unlikely to happen for them.

By comparison, in the same study, couples who were more open to gender equity and the economic and family benefits that a breadwinning wife could offer tended to be highly educated and both likely to have spent time in managerial positions.

When these financially better-off couples had children, they had larger families but spent less time on individual childcare, getting help from childcare providers. They also spent less time on housework, again using their money to buy support.[42] Indeed, many of the women I spent time with used a variety of support mechanisms including family members, nurseries, nannies, child-minders as well as food delivery services and paid cleaners.

NAVIGATING THE TUMULTUOUS TURNING TIDE

This departure from the norm is necessary – but those who publicly recognise the changing tide are often criticised.

Cartoonist David Horsey received harsh criticism for a Father's Day sketch entitled *The Sign of the Times* which he drew in a *Seattle Post* newspaper. The sketch featured a small girl looking up to her beer-drinking despondent-looking father and asking: 'Since you lost your job and Mom is supporting us, should I just give my Father's Day card to her?'

He responded to the furore by pointing out that his job as a cartoonist is to be controversial and poke fun at changing social dynamics. Horsey explains: 'My cartoon may have been a little raw, but it wasn't all that far off target. American men are entering a new era where the old assumptions about their place in society are being challenged as never before. This is not necessarily bad, but for some guys it will not be easy.'[43]

As David Horsey discovered, the increase in the number of women who are not only earning but out-earning their partners has indeed been difficult for some men to accept. Naila Kabeer, of the University of Sussex, explained global perspectives on the emerging role of women as primary breadwinners:

---

[42] Drago, R, Black, D, Wooden, M (2004) 'Female Breadwinner Families: Their Existence, Persistence and Sources', Melbourne Institute Working Paper, August 2004
[43] http://blog.seattlepi.com/davidhorsey/archives/211969.asp

'Resistance to this change is 'mainly in their roles as husbands rather than as fathers, brothers or sons... Male identity and power relations are far more closely bound up with the appearance, if not face, of women's financial dependence within marriage. The complex negotiations through which women and men are attempting to come to terms with women's increasingly visible role as breadwinners is leading to unexpected reconfigurations of personal and family life across the global economy...

'Consequently, many women appear to be pursuing strategies of 'wielding and yielding', *making concessions and compromises* in order to take up paid work without jeopardising their marriages.

'Continued responsibility for a major share of unpaid domestic work, including care of children and the elderly, appears to be the *most* frequent concession yielded by women. They are permitted to go out to work as long as their husbands are not required to shoulder a greater share of this unpaid labour. On the other hand, not all women are willing to accept the unfairness of this compromise. Some have used their newfound earning power to renegotiate unsatisfactory marital relationships, forcing some degree of change in the division of domestic responsibilities.

'Others have left to set up their own households with children, leading to rising rates of female households across the world. Such households are often poorer on average than others but their children are not necessarily more disadvantaged, since their mothers have greater control over the use of their earnings.[44]

'As women in more prosperous countries move up the occupational ladder, it is women from the poorer countries of the world who have responded to this rising demand for paid help in the home.'

But it requires time away from their own children to come to richer countries and look after another woman's children: 'It is generally *their own mothers* rather than their husbands who take care of their children during these absences.' Mothers who are also the primary breadwinners certainly face an uphill struggle in the workplace.

---

[44] Kabeer, N (2008) 'Marriage, Motherhood and Masculinity in the Global Economy', University of Sussex, January 29, www.opendemocracy.net

WHY HER FIRST SALARY COUNTS

The average American woman in full-time employment loses $434,000 in income over a 40-year period due to the gender pay gap[45]. For women with more education, it's even greater. Women with at least a university degree lose up to $713,000 over that 40-year period made up from the cumulative effects of lower starting salaries and their related benefits.

This pay gap accumulates for a variety of reasons, but chief among them is that pay rises are typically given as a percentage of *current* salary, leaving women further behind each year. A new employer will typically ask a job applicant for a salary history when determining his or her starting salary, which further limits women's upward mobility.[46] These figures don't even take into account part-time workers where the disparity is even greater.

Certainly, women are twice as likely as men to be in part-time employment. Since few jobs offer part-time flexibility, they tend to pay disproportionately less because there is greater demand for them – but in reality this does not explain fully the gap in pay discussed above.

It is important to note that a gender pay gap exists in the first year that women graduate from university, at a point in their lives when differences in work experience between them and their male colleagues cannot realistically play a large part in determining pay.

The American Association of University Women found that women who go to the same kind of university, with the same degree, getting the same job with similar workplace flexibility perks, and who have the same personal characteristics – such as age, race and number of children – still earn five per cent less than their male colleagues in their *first* year of work alone.

Ten years later, even if the women have not taken a break for childrearing and kept pace with their male colleagues, this widens to 12 per cent.[47] Clearly, the gap cannot be conveniently blamed on the 'lifestyle choices' a woman has made.

---

[45] Arons, J (2008) 'Lifetime Losses: The Career Wage Gap' Center for American Progress
[46] Wenger, J (2001) 'The Continuing Problem with Part-time Jobs', Washington: Economic Policy Institute
[47] American Association of University Women (2007) 'Behind the Pay Gap'

There has been progress, and recent research has demonstrated that the pay gap in the UK is at its lowest point ever for full-time workers, now at just 10 per cent for full-time workers and 20 per cent for all workers in all categories.[48]

Similarly, the US Bureau of Labor Statistics reported that the wage gap between men and women has narrowed so dramatically that it is now the smallest on record. There is even evidence that young women under 30 in many metropolitan cities are earning slightly more than men their own age. In the US, single, childless women in their twenties now earn eight per cent more than their male peers.[49] The UK's Office for National Statistics found similar disparity favouring young women.

However, before we congratulate ourselves on pay equality achieved, this is not real evidence of long-term pay equality that continues as these women age. Instead, it is due to the widening gap between the academic achievement of young men and women today. There are simply *more* women working in professional occupations than men in the same age bracket, which is why the average earnings for women of this age group surpass those of their male counterparts.

Additionally, recent recessionary job losses from many traditionally male industries, such as financial services and construction, play a part. Indeed, this 'equality' stops as women enter their thirties and begin to have children, at which point the pay gap significantly penalises working women over the age of 40 who, according to ONS data, take home only 73 per cent of male earnings.

---

[48] UK Office for National Statistics (2010) 'Annual Survey of Hours and Earnings'
[49] US Bureau of Labor Statistics (March 2010) 'Women at Work'

> *Married men are better off financially than ever before, due to the gains of their wives.*
>
> •
>
> *Highly educated couples are most likely to use the female breadwinner model successfully.*
>
> •
>
> *Young childless women now out-earn men their own age.*

WHY MUM GETS PAID LESS THAN DAD

The picture is particularly stark for working mothers who indeed face more workplace bias. Researchers at Cornell University compared people's perceptions of fictional male and female job candidates, some of whom were parents, some not. Incredibly, despite identical credentials for all the fictional candidates, mothers were seen as less competent, less likely to be recommended for management, less likely to be recommended for selection, less promotable and had lower recommended starting salaries.

Fathers, however, were not seen negatively. In fact, perceptions of working fathers were slightly boosted, no doubt related to the expectations we have of men as responsible breadwinners.[50] Employers need to recognise that a large proportion of working mothers are also the main earners.

This backs up other research finding that interruptions from work, working part-time and decreased seniority explain no more than about one third of the pay gap between women with and without children.[51] Two thirds of the pay gap must be because of the discrimination against working mothers.

---

[50] Correll, S, Benard, S, Paik, I (2007) 'Getting a job: Is there a motherhood penalty?', *The American Journal of Sociology*, 112 (5) 1297–1338

[51] Budig, MJ & England, P (2001) 'The Wage Penalty for Motherhood', *American Sociological Review*, 66 (2)

While some might argue working mothers are less productive, most working mothers I know are amazed at how much more productive they become after having children. They simply no longer have time to waste. They work through lunch and become masters of multi-tasking. I believe their supposed downfall is not that they are less committed to their careers, but they are just less willing to devote hours to the politicking and networking that are so important to career success in the modern workplace.

Perhaps not surprisingly, mothers who work full-time tend to be better educated than other mothers.[52] Since these women will command a premium for their expertise, the higher opportunity costs of *not* working make full-time employment all the more attractive. However, it is not education alone that makes the difference in whether or not a woman will continue to work after the birth of a child. Rather, it is whether she is the main breadwinner for her growing family.

Interestingly, among new mothers, being the primary breadwinner is far more of an incentive to work than just being better educated than their partners. According to recent research by Shireen Kanji at the University of Cambridge who looked at women who had recently become mothers, those whose annual earnings are at least 20 per cent higher than their partner's are four times as likely to continue working full-time as mothers who are minor earners in relation to their partner.[53]

Iceland, which has the most generous paternity leave legislation in the world (three months), not surprisingly also has the smallest wage gap between men and women. Employers find it hard to discriminate against women of childbearing age, knowing that their male employees are just as likely to take leave for child-raising.

If men in other countries were to embrace parental leave, the wage gap would probably decrease further. Plus, working women would be spared the stigma of the 'mummy track' and the professional doubt and penalties that too often accompany the

---

[52] Rubery, J et al (1999) 'Women's Employment in Europe: Trends and Prospects, London, Routledge
[53] Kanji, S (2010) 'What keeps mothers in full-time employment?', European Sociological Review

label. The rise of the female breadwinner means that addressing the gender pay gap is all the more vital. Many women are the main financial provider for their families, whether there is a man at home or not.

Almost half (46 per cent) of the breadwinning wives surveyed by *Redbook* magazine in 2010 said that they and their husbands were equally happy with the arrangement; interestingly, a further 30 per cent suspected they were happier with it than their husbands were. Just a third (35 per cent) said they wished their partner would take more responsibility for earning more. Notably, the majority said they would not trade salaries with their husbands.[54]

A MARATHON, NOT A SPRINT

Some of the female breadwinners I spoke to came from a long line of working women; others had had mothers who had stayed at home. As one woman whose mother and aunt had been primary breadwinners in their own homes in the 1950s exclaims: 'I always had this feeling *you had better be prepared!* It was quite clear growing up that you couldn't always rely on a man!'

Most women anticipated that their role as primary breadwinner would continue, in some cases for several more years, in other cases until they retired. Only a small handful thought their partner might eventually earn more than them. Interestingly, this was not because the model of *female* breadwinning was untenable or unattractive.

Rather, any expectation that they might switch earnings with their partners was due to just two things: an anticipation that their partners' businesses would become profitable *or* a realisation that the *hours* the women put in to earn well were unsustainable in the long run.

Katrina, who is 44 and works on Wall Street, says: 'Sometimes I think Simon would like me to retire because he doesn't like to

---

[54] Goad, K (2010) 'Big earning wives, and the men who love them', *MSN Lifestyle*, September 13

see me working so hard. I don't know how many more years I can work these types of hours. I have been in the business long enough to see the effects of burnout.' Like Barbara, a woman we will meet, who suffered a life-threatening bleeding ulcer, stress plays a real part in the long-term considerations of many of these women

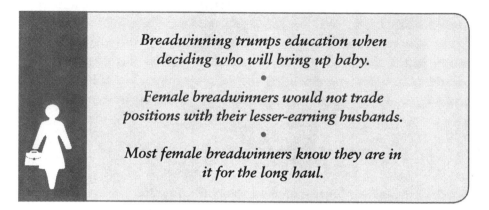

Breadwinning trumps education when deciding who will bring up baby.

•

Female breadwinners would not trade positions with their lesser-earning husbands.

•

Most female breadwinners know they are in it for the long haul.

THE MYTH OF MR MOM

So how do these non-traditional, but increasingly common families manage? The conflict for men comes, as it has done for women, in balancing work and family needs. Women taking on a greater share of the breadwinning are asking for more help, and many men are indeed answering the call.

I am reluctant to call fathers who are the primary caregivers of their children 'stay-at-home' dads, simply because so many do not *stay at home*. Even if they have no paid work, just like mothers they *go out* to shops, to the park, play groups, story time at the library or even for a well-earned coffee.

Equally, like women who work part-time or from a home-based office, most of the partners of breadwinning wives would not be classified as a 'stay-at-home' dad because of their multi-layered identities. They make an effort to define themselves with other roles: web designer, freelance writer, consultant, entrepreneur.

Furthermore, the 'Mister Mom' tag is over-simplistic and patronising, giving the impression that fathers are masquerading as women and doing a 'mother's work'.[55] The term can also do a disservice to men who believe in gender equality and view competence in child-rearing and household tasks as a commitment to their families and what it means to be a good partner and father, not a second rate version of 'Mom'.

THE REALITY OF THE DAD-AT-HOME

An Aviva survey found that now more than 600,000 UK men, or six per cent of men with dependent children, look after their children while their wife or girlfriend works. This is a stunning tenfold increase since 2000. A further 18 per cent of parents say that they share childcare equally in their household. Certainly, I would imagine a larger acceptance of men in the childcare role has led more men openly and proudly to claim their part in childcare.

The same study found men's attitudes are rapidly changing too. Three quarters (75 per cent) of at-home dads feel *lucky* to be spending time with their children, and 29 per cent find looking after children *more* rewarding than going out to work. Indeed childcare suits them, as only 10 per cent felt that looking after their children made them 'less of a man.' Similarly, less than one in five (17 per cent) wished they earned more so that their partner could stay at home.[56] Clearly men in the at-home role are far happier than we might expect.

This shift does not come without challenges, particularly for women. Of breadwinning women, 37 per cent feel guilty going out to work and leaving their children; and one in seven say they occasionally resent their male partner because they have to go out to work. However, while the myth that 'women want to be at home' persists, less than one in ten women (nine per cent) would actually swap places with their partner to become the stay-at-home parent. Clearly, while women may experience moments of doubt, the majority of female breadwinners are happy to work.

[55] Gerson, K (1993) *No Man's Land: Men's Changing Commitments to Family and Work*, New York, Basic Books

[56] Aviva press release 'Ten Times More Stay-at-home Dads than Ten Years Ago', 7 April 2010

WILL THE MODERN MAN PLEASE STEP FORWARD?

Even people not reliant on female income are becoming more accepting of working mothers. The percentage of all men who agree 'it's better for all involved if the man earns the money and the woman takes care of the home and children' dropped significantly from 74 per cent in 1977 to 42 per cent in 2008.

Additionally, the number of men agreeing that 'a mother who works outside the home can have just as good a relationship with her children as a mother who does not work' has increased significantly from 49 per cent in 1977 to 67 per cent in 2008, with the most significant changes amongst older men over the age of 63.[57]

I suspect those older men are now proudly watching their well-educated daughters work for pay and raise families. Certainly, when I talk to men about the work I do in helping develop female leaders, older men with grown daughters of their own are some of the staunchest supporters of women in the workplace. They want to believe their bright daughters can 'have it all'.

This rapid change shows striking shifts in the way men feel about gender, work and parenting. Jackie left teaching for a more lucrative and varied career in marketing. She says that while her father raised her with high expectations, her mother was 'horrified' when she wanted to go to university. She had hoped Jackie would marry early and have children.

When they married, Donald was a chemist and they earned equally. The same year, he was offered a high profile job in Singapore with his employer. The company refused to allow Jackie, his new wife, to accompany him. Instead of taking this type of 'promotion', Donald resigned. She laughs: 'It was crazy because I went to his farewell party at work, and people asked me, "how can you stand in the way of his success?" They conveniently overlooked the fact that their refusal to let me accompany him was the main issue!'

---

[57] Galinsky, E et al (2009) 'Times are Changing: Gender and Generation at Work and at Home', Families and Work Institute

Jackie's own employer, on the other hand, was very flexible. Fearing that she would accompany her husband to Singapore, they asked if Donald would be willing to leave chemistry and retrain as an accountant working for them. Even Jackie was surprised when he agreed, and he happily worked for the company for many years. Her company's flexibility should be a model for other employers looking to retain talent, whether male or female.

When their first son was born, they used the on-site employer's crèche and Donald considered leaving work for good. Their company was so keen to keep Donald, however, they suggested he work part-time at home and installed remote computer access. This change suited him since Donald had never liked the daily managerial aspects of the job.

Jackie says: 'There was no big debate as to whether or not one of us would stay at home. Donald was never as ambitious as me. Plus, the company bent over backwards to accommodate him, requiring him in London just one day a month. If I had stayed in teaching and he in chemistry, I might have been the one at home since it would have made the most financial sense to do so. Even if he had risen higher as a chemist, I doubt he could have ever matched what I was bringing home before I retired.'

Donald, who may have seemed like a pioneering father at the time, is certainly not alone. A recent report from the charity Working Families found most working fathers (82 per cent) would like more family time. They also found that the perceptions of working fathers are rapidly changing. In fact, fewer fathers than mothers agreed with the statement that 'it is a mother's role to look after children'.

Perhaps as a result of the additional family time they are putting in, fathers are feeling more stressed than they have historically been, but those fathers who do more housework are *less stressed* than those who do less. Additionally, fathers whose partners work full-time have a better sense of well-being than those whose partners only work part-time.[58] It may be that the partnerships

---

[58] Gattrell, C (2010) Working Families and Lancaster University School of Management 'Work Life Balance: Working for Fathers?' www.workingfamilies.org.uk

where chores are split more fairly are benefiting from an enhanced sense of *teamwork*. The face of the modern workforce is rapidly changing, with more employees wanting time at home.

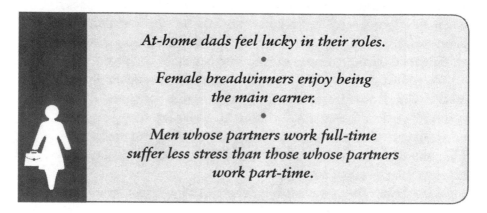

At-home dads feel lucky in their roles.

•

Female breadwinners enjoy being the main earner.

•

Men whose partners work full-time suffer less stress than those whose partners work part-time.

REINVENTING THE FAMILY

I have long suspected we will see one of two family models emerge. The first model features more men taking the home-making role, to provide childcare and the general running of day-to-day family life. In this model the full-time worker of a couple is not determined primarily by gender but by earnings potential, an area in which women are fast gaining ground. These couples will be pragmatic and will choose roles according to interest and capability – not according to prescriptive gender roles.

The drawback to this model is that it requires both partners in a couple to work long hours but doing entirely different things. One will focus on domestic work with little if any employment experience; the other will be putting in long hours at paid work in order to be the primary wage earner. They will become very dependent on each other and the arrangement will only work well if they are both completely fulfilled in their individual roles.

As an alternative to that model, I'd like to offer a more egalitarian, yet radical proposal. In this model, the *workplace* changes to allow greater autonomy and flexibility for *all* workers: male or female. No worker is pushed to work more than a manageable workload. Extreme jobs and the burnout that often accompanies them would be a thing of the past.

This would enable both partners to enjoy the intellectual stimulation of work as well as the responsibilities and pleasures of a home life. It would give employers the benefit of a workforce that is made up of *most* of the population, rather than just those who are prepared to give the lion's share of their waking hours to work.

The challenge inherent in this model is that it would take a systematic restructuring of the modern workplace. Values would need to shift towards a results-based workforce rather than an hours-based workforce. Men and women would have to accept duality in their roles and responsibilities but the benefits in so doing could massively enhance society and people's enjoyment of each sphere.

Government can also do more to legitimise the role of fathers. Extending paternity benefits, as part of a parenting leave, would be a good way to encourage greater gender parity in the workplace. Because parenting leave is so heavily weighted towards the role of mothers, maternity leave encourages families to think of post-birth caring as primarily the woman's responsibility. There are several negative implications of this focus.

In the first instance, fathers who take no or only minimal leave can become remote from young babies, as we will discuss. Secondly, employers are more likely to be wary of hiring young women of childbearing years for fear of lengthy and multiple maternity leaves. Clearly, the answer is not extending maternity leave, as governments have considered, but in encouraging men to take a greater share of the leave time available.

If parenting leave was extended by several months, *but only for fathers willing to take paternity leave,* employers would no longer be so biased against hiring women. Employers would recognise that prospective male employees with growing families were as likely to take paternity leave as women. This move would enable female breadwinners to get back to work quicker and allow men to bond with their young children in a way that serves their families and society far better.

EQUALITY AT HOME:
VARYING CROSS-CULTURAL PERSPECTIVES

In many parts of the world, women's increased earnings mean an increased voice in the family politics.

As explained the *American Journal of Sociology*: 'In parts of Kenya for example, men's initial reluctance to their wives' independent trading activities often diminishes in the face of *the incomes* the women were able to bring home. In light of the diminished self-esteem, frustrations at their own declining position can give rise to hostile behaviour. Some husbands simply left to set up households with other women or returned to their natal home where they could be looked after by their mothers or sisters.

'Others used their wives' entry into paid employment as a pretext to withdraw their own contributions, choosing unemployment over low status work. Others have resorted to appropriating their wives' earnings, domestic violence and extramarital affairs in an attempt to exert their own authority in the household.'[59]

Perhaps not surprisingly, exemption from unpaid domestic chores appears to be the privilege men most strongly defend. The division of unpaid domestic labour becomes a flashpoint in the negotiation process as to whether the woman will work, or indeed how many hours she is 'allowed' to work outside the home.

Men were less likely to object to their wives working outside the home if they themselves were not expected to do more housework and childcare. A Chilean study of working couples found men more willing to take on domestic chores *if* their wives earned at least double their income and if the men were relatively young and had been raised in the habit of doing household chores.[60]

Indeed, far from taking on more of the household maintenance, many men eschew these responsibilities precisely at the time when they could offer more support. There is evidence that as a man becomes economically dependent on his wife, the amount of

---

[59] Francis, E (2002) 'Gender, migration and multiple livelihoods: Cases from Eastern and Southern Africa', *The Journal of Development Studies*, 38 (5), 167–190

[60] Alméras, Diane (2000) 'Equitable social practices and masculine personal history: A Santiago study', *European Journal of Development Research*, 12 (2), 139–153

housework he does actually *decreases.*[61]

Similarly, Australian research has found that in couples where women earn more than half of the family income, they often retain or return to the traditional gendered divisions of home labour.[62]

Allison Holland, a South African management consultant, agrees: 'Actually, my husband is not so bothered about childcare, but he hates the housework. We have a cleaner come in and do the cleaning twice a month. South Africa is much more traditional, and housework is definitely a woman's responsibility, and I think that affects us both.'

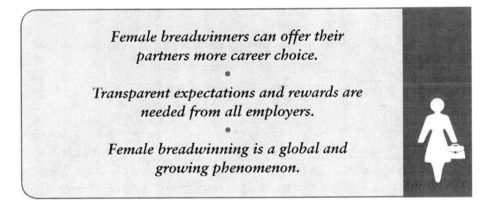

Female breadwinners can offer their partners more career choice.

•

Transparent expectations and rewards are needed from all employers.

•

Female breadwinning is a global and growing phenomenon.

[61] Brines, J (1994) 'Economic dependency, gender and the division of labor at home', *American Journal of Sociology*, 100, 652–688

[62] Batman, M et al (2003) 'When does gender trump money? Bargaining and time in household work', *American Journal of Sociology*, 109, 186–214

3

WHY COUPLES DEPART
FROM THE NORM

'Sexual politics in the workplace is easy compared to sexual politics in your own kitchen.'

VICKI WOODS

Some couples I spoke to were pragmatic about their choices, having decided early on that it would be best to devote their energies to her career rather than his. Others used a turning point to identify when the time was right for her to become the primary breadwinner. These turning points took many forms: a lay-off, illness, birth of a child, relocation or even the threat of terrorism.

What they had in common was the realisation that it would be wisest to follow her career as it had the most potential or was best for their current family situation. They were practical about what would work best. Their goal was simply to create a home where both partners could flourish in their roles.

TERRORISM AND ITS UNEXPECTED EFFECTS

As a sign of the modern times, several female breadwinners cited the terrorist attacks of 9/11 in New York and the Underground bombings in London on July 7 as watershed moments for their families. These events put what the women wanted from family life into sharp focus. They served as epiphanies for how they and their husbands wanted to live: with less stress and more focus on what was best for their children.

Katrina, a senior executive working on Wall Street, was one such woman. She met her husband Simon more than 20 years ago on the commuter train when they were both just a few weeks out of university. Simon also initially worked in banking but eventually left to move into sales. Katrina is very respectful of his capability as a sales person but explains: 'His pay was always so variable. In sales you eat what you kill. I, on the other hand, am much more methodical, doing my MBA at night, always building, but never strategically creating a career.'

Simon did very well in his sales career, working at six or seven different companies before becoming international sales manager with a retail firm. She recalls: 'We had two beautiful children and enjoyed our careers, but were working crazy hours and getting the support we needed from two different nannies. Everything changed on 9/11. I was next door to the World Trade Centre when the buildings went down. As you can imagine, walking out of those buildings was one of the most traumatic moments of my life.'

She continues: 'Over the next few months Simon and I began to consider *What the hell are we doing?* We wanted another child, but he was travelling internationally most weeks and I was working crazy hours in Manhattan. I remember the alarm clock going off one morning so that he could take a transatlantic flight to London. The newscaster announced "white powder warnings" [purported to be the anthrax virus used as a biological weapon] and to travel only if absolutely necessary.'

She sighs: 'We basically had a "come to Jesus" moment where we realised that while we both loved our jobs, something had to change.' That year was particularly difficult for them as a family. They lost both her parents and his mother within the nine months surrounding 9/11. Katrina elaborates: 'At a relatively early stage in the life of our family, we had to take stock of what life is all about.'

The couple decided to capitalise on Simon's passion for teaching, a dream he had initially relegated to retirement. Katrina explains:

'I absolutely love my work and I don't have any other burning passions. I love my children, but I don't think I'd be a great full-time mom. We didn't want Simon to stop working. He has enormous professional pride and enjoys meeting people too much to leave that behind, but we knew something had to change. He'd always talked about getting into teaching and we thought, *why wait?*'

This change meant Katrina could continue to work demanding hours and Simon could find a fulfilling role closer to home and be around for their children. After much planning, they made the switch when their third child was born.

She remembers: 'Before going for it, we talked a lot about this. Let's face it, as a starting teacher you are not going to make a lot of money. Our only other option was me to stay at home, but I was just starting to out-earn him at that point and we were optimistic about my career prospects at the firm. More importantly, I didn't see myself as a stay-at-home mom. His passion for teaching made the decision easy.'

IN SICKNESS AND IN HEALTH

When people consider the conditions that lead to a woman taking on the breadwinning role, they often think of some type of disabling illness that means a man can't physically work. This certainly occurred, but these couples were in the minority.

Myra and Derek met and married as postgraduate students at Oxford. At age 23 and just a few weeks before their wedding, Derek was diagnosed with ME (Myalgic Encephalopathy) or Chronic Fatigue Syndrome. It became severe so rapidly that he attended their wedding in a wheelchair. No doubt this would have been a complete shock to any young couple.

Nevertheless, Derek was awarded a post-doctoral research fellowship in Physics, then a lectureship, and was able to recover sufficiently to work at a university throughout his twenties. His illness returned along with the pressure he felt in finding funding for his department. By the age of 30, Derek was forced to retire on a disability pension.

From the moment this happened, Myra knew her career path was never going to be straightforward. She realised the burden of earning would always lie with her. While Derek receives a pension from the university, for most of their relationship Myra has brought home the lion's share of the family income.

She remembers: 'His early retirement was a massive drain on me. Suddenly I had to take my career much more seriously.' Myra had spent her twenties as a research scientist. However, after Derek's retirement, she then took on a more remunerative position as a chemist within the private sector.

The situation for Derek was extremely frustrating as he was still as mentally agile as ever. She says: 'The upside is that he's been able to travel with me for work.' She laughs: 'Plus he's been able to read all the books we dream of having the time to read! His health fluctuates, and while he's doing better now, I don't think he'll ever be suited to full-time work.

'He's interested in blogging and writing, but what do you write about if you have been ill for so long: illness? He doesn't want to be defined by his diagnosis. He's so articulate I think he'd be a great advocate, helping others to understand the illness. Not many people, even doctors, fully comprehend it. It's seen as *laziness*, not a *real disease*, but I can tell you as someone who lives with it every day – it is real.'

Ironically, Derek has almost achieved the academic's life he wanted. He's widely-read and even wrote a book on the Aboriginal peoples of Australia which was subsequently turned down by several publishers. It took him several years to complete, but he only submitted the work to publishers after it had become a 900-page opus.

Myra says: 'This is our one bone of contention. I recently wrote a four-page book proposal on my line of work and was offered a contract from the first publisher I approached. That certainly caused some resentment. He wouldn't take my advice to approach a publisher first with the idea.'

Judy and Ian are another such couple, where his illness has forced her to take on the responsibility of breadwinning. Judy is a pharmaceuticals executive and her husband is a research scientist.

Early on, he earned more, but she caught up after a series of promotions. Because Ian's research area was so specialist, they chose to live where he could find work, confident that Judy could find work locally. Some years he earned more, some years she earned more. These moves took them all over Europe, and, by the time I interviewed her, they were based in Italy.

Judy has only become the breadwinner in the last four years, after Ian was diagnosed with a terminal illness. She says: 'I don't think the money is terribly important to him because, based on what he wanted to achieve with his life, he's done it. I think if you are in a less satisfying job, then perhaps money is more important. He's proud because he's done groundbreaking research in his life. But he is frustrated now, not so much because he isn't *earning* but because he isn't *working*. His work now is in getting better and that's hard for him.'

Understandably, the stress on Judy is high. When Ian was diagnosed, she was in a more junior role, and felt an immediate pressure to stay in a job she wanted to leave. This was particularly difficult during a period of redundancies that swept through the company. She sighs: 'I can't hide the fact that there are redundancies since it's all over the media. But I won't tell him how scared I was. That's a very different thing. I had to be strong for him.'

When asked how the change in their circumstances has affected their relationship, she answers: 'The balance is gone. I knew I could rely on him financially and vice versa. It's hard because this is permanent. The truth is he won't get better and I have the responsibility for us going forward. We don't have quite the same honesty now between us. I know men must have had this responsibility for eons, so I can't complain.

'It's hard to turn down any request from work because I need the job so much. He's getting chemotherapy now so I don't like to travel. But with the threat of redundancies hanging over my head, I know I have to play the game. I no longer have the choice to do anything else.'

BEING HEALTHY, WEALTHY AND WISE

Some couples found that illness for *her* shed new light on the breadwinning situation.

Vashti, an airport security specialist, is still the main breadwinner but feels less career-driven than in the past. A few years ago she contracted breast cancer and subsequently opted to hand over her management responsibilities. She now works four and a half days a week. By the time of our interview, her husband, Terence, had similarly given notice on a project he was overseeing that required him to be in Germany most weeks.

She explains: 'The cancer changed our perspective. Terence is still ambitious, but I'm no longer so driven. I want to spend time with our son, James. Working my way up the ladder isn't as appealing as it once was.' Not all health scares for women ended so positively, nor indeed with greater choice for the future.

Barbara, a private banker, was diagnosed with a bleeding intestinal tumour while on a Christmas holiday with her children and parents. She was slowly bleeding to death. She sighs: 'It was all very dramatic and they weren't even sure I would make it through the operation. I called Heinrich, who was back in Austria, and asked him to pick up the children. He came to California where I was in hospital, but he was fairly uncommunicative and left with them for Vienna on the same day. When I recuperated, friends told me that in the weeks following, "Heinrich was very worried" – not about my health, but about what would happen to our income if I died.'

Barbara's husband, Heinrich, organises adventure holidays in Africa, but the company barely breaks even, so he doesn't contribute to the financial running of the household. She says: 'I thought maybe this would be the wake-up call Heinrich needed to see we can't completely rely on me. We'd have to take care of each other. The doctors had said the tumour was stress-induced and I wanted Heinrich to see I can't keep up this pace forever. Unfortunately, he doesn't appear to have come to that realisation.'

She says: 'I'm not sure being the main earner can work long term for women. I think women need to feel loved and cared for. There is a financial aspect to that, but I don't think inherently women want to be on top. They might have to be strong in their working lives, but there is always a softer side to women. It's impossible to stay on top all the time. You want a *partnership*, and I don't have a partnership.'

So, what *do* men want? Barbara pauses: 'I think they have the same needs and desires. I'm very close to all of my male colleagues. At work they need to feel that they're on top, but they also require their wives to be supportive and self-sufficient. Perhaps not financially self-sufficient, because the city breeds a different type of male, but in their private life.'

When asked more about what breed of men the city cultivates she says: 'They get bored easily. They like a fast pace, very driven and money-focused. That's not what I wanted for Heinrich, but any type of self-sufficiency would be nice. I might get a card at my birthday, but that's it. If he gets me something, I am paying for it. After a while it takes its toll and I don't ever think it is going to change.' She continues: 'The downside is that there is no one ever saying, "You look tired, let's go out for dinner" or, "I saw this gift and thought you would love it".'

Heinrich also does not help with the children or housework. For Barbara, it is clear that the issue is not money, but the lack of any reciprocity; the mark of a true partnership. Though Barbara speaks in a calm tone throughout her entire interview, it's clear that the experience was as painful for her emotionally as it had been physically. The whole experience gave Barbara time to reflect. Unfortunately she found the experience of being the breadwinner unfulfilling because of the lack of reciprocity.

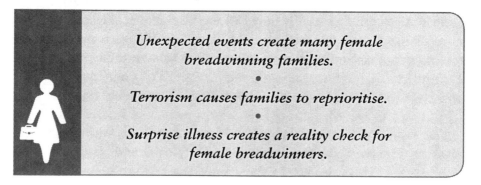

Unexpected events create many female breadwinning families.

•

Terrorism causes families to reprioritise.

•

Surprise illness creates a reality check for female breadwinners.

THE SILVER LINING TO REDUNDANCIES

Redundancies rarely come at a good time, but for some they can give couples the opportunity to contemplate a new way of living. Melanie and Connor took that opportunity. They were initially colleagues in their first jobs after university. Before they married, Connor left work to go back to university for a Master's degree, and Melanie supported them both. She says: 'His degree was always going to be an investment in our future.'

After his degree was finished, Connor went back to work. Unfortunately, he was made redundant several times while Melanie began to progress up the ladder in her job within the automotive industry. She says: 'Connor works in HR, which is always subject to budget cuts.' Connor then worked in a series of interim positions.

Melanie remembers: 'On the first day of one of his new roles, he was told his main responsibility would be to fire everyone else. Then he had to do the clean-up paperwork and shut the door on his own way out!' Needless to say, these roles did not give Connor the job satisfaction he wanted.

When their third child was starting school, his company was bought out. This time he raised the option of voluntary redundancy and opted to take a career break. A family friend had taken a year out of a stressful banking job and recommended it as life-changing. The change made sense since they found the daily school run for three children completely exhausting. Melanie said the breaking point came when she was recommended anti-depressants by her doctor because of the stress she was under.

She recalls: 'I realised the answer did not involve drugs, so I went to a therapist. She asked me to write down everything we did in a week. She said she needed to lie down after just reading it!' The therapist was a useful sounding board for Melanie. She realised they were taking too much on and that the stress was not a sign of any personal failing, but an indication that their dual workloads were unsustainable.

Connor opted to take a year out, initially to help the family cope better. Melanie explains: 'I knew we could make it work if he wanted to completely stop. He was under a great deal of pressure from his mother to be The Provider and he does take time to mull things over. I knew he would have to come to the decision to quit for good on his own, which he did.'

Saying nothing, even when it was obvious to Melanie they would be better served in the long run if he stopped work, was probably one of the key factors in his decision. *Insisting* he leave the workforce would have created a huge backlash from him. After trying out the arrangement for several months, he came to the decision himself that he would like to be at home more permanently.

Melanie says: 'He struggled in the role at first because he wondered what other people would think. It's made a huge difference that he's been able to volunteer with our children's school and use his HR knowledge. He loves it because it gets him out of the house and the headteacher was smart enough to see he could review remuneration packages, staff training and appraisal systems, all for free.'

She continues: 'He's now a governor of the school, which is pretty good for someone who is naturally introverted. When people ask what he does, he will say he's a house husband, but quickly follow up with the fact that he's also the chairman of governors for our school.'

Obviously, the dual sense of identity is vital for Connor. In fact, she agrees with the suggestion that his official role at the school also makes is easier for him to say he's a stay-at-home father. Melanie is clear that it is the *status* he now enjoys which makes the difference. He goes to the school several times a week, and it gives him something to talk with Melanie about on a professional level, which has also improved their relationship.

When she looks at the benefits Connor's role over the last several years has brought their three children, Melanie remarks: 'They are much more confident now. They all just love the fact that their dad is there. They don't care that it's their dad versus their mum. I take our two daughters out for girly stuff at the weekends, but they've never said it's odd that it's Connor at home and not me.'

Melanie says: 'I sometimes think Connor loses sight of how

important he is to us in the scheme of things. I remind him that I couldn't do any of this without him and that he has utterly changed the kids' lives for the better. I will often compliment him when I know he is in earshot.'

Connor's decision to stay at home has increased Melanie's confidence at work. Accordingly, she has just been promoted to a role liaising between the automotive industry and the national government. Friends might say to her: 'So, Melanie, which politicians did you see on your way to Whitehall today?' Then they jokingly add: 'And how many coffee mornings have you gone to, Connor?'

Melanie smiles: 'They know it winds him up. I will agree that, yes, my job can be exciting at times, but I couldn't do it without Connor. I feel like I need to sometimes remind people this isn't a social experiment and we've actually got a great life. There is no way I could have done this role when we were both working. It is just too demanding. But now I know that Connor's handling everything at home, so I don't have to give it a second thought.'

She advises: 'Don't listen to people who talk about everything that can go wrong. Deal with the issues as they arise rather than assuming it won't work. Also, it's taboo for people to talk about women out-earning men, but if enough people talk about it, it will gradually become normal. That can only help. It's like the concept of *working mothers*. It will become commonplace for couples to not assume it will always be the woman at home.'

THE LUXURY OF CHOICE

Part of the success Connor had in transitioning to the at-home role is no doubt related to the feeling that he had a *choice*. Not all couples are so lucky. Sometimes a job loss forces a woman to be the main breadwinner and the man to take a supporting role, whether he wants to or not.

Maureen and Bill have been married for fifteen years and have a pre-teen daughter. Maureen is an entrepreneur with a successful PR business, and now brings home 80 per cent of the family income. When they first met, Maureen, who is Scottish, worked in Edinburgh.

Bill was the director of a commercial heating business in Manchester. Because he was an equity partner with 35 per cent ownership in the business, they decided it made sense for Maureen to move to Manchester. She negotiated with her employer to go freelance and set up her PR agency in Manchester to handle accounts they gave her. She says: 'I don't think of myself as a risk-taker. If the circumstances hadn't forced my move, I don't think I would have ever left full-time employment. I wouldn't have done it without Bill pushing me.'

Establishing the business was difficult, and for several years she paid her employees more than herself just to keep it going. Fifteen years on, the business now turns over a million pounds a year. She is a successful business woman, and it is from Maureen that I learned the mantra of all solvent business owners: *Turnover is vanity, profit is sanity!*

Before they married, however, Bill's salary was double hers. Maureen says: 'We openly joke about how the tables have really turned. We have a total role reversal.'

Unfortunately, Bill didn't have a choice about who was the main breadwinner; his at-home role was thrust upon him. Just a week after they married, his business partner secretly sold his shares to a large competitor, essentially making Bill redundant overnight. Maureen remembers: 'That was a horrible shock to the system, and understandably Bill took it very badly. Not only did he lose his job, but also his sense of identity and his trust in a chap whom he'd thought was his best friend.

'What was worse, Bill had no other qualifications, having worked his way up in the business over the previous ten years. He'd grown it from nothing to a turnover of more than fifteen million pounds. It was utterly devastating.'

Bill found the whole experience demoralising and had no interest in building a company from scratch again. As Maureen points out: 'Since he'd been managing director, he was used to working for himself. It's hard working for someone else after you have been your own boss.'

At this point, Maureen was still building her business and barely taking home a salary. The money they received from the buy-out, roughly equivalent to eighteen months' salary, helped cushion them temporarily.

Maureen is quick to credit Bill through this period. 'He's amazing. He always is willing to work. He went from being an MD to driving trucks, which replaced almost half his salary. It was hard work for several years before then deciding to turn his hobby of writing into a freelance job, which he does off and on. He brings in some money but it's not a lot.'

So, how did they get through the difficult years? She says: 'The darkest time was when I was working crazy hours building the business. I was not earning much, just praying that it would succeed. I would come home and he'd *still* criticise me for what I wasn't doing right at home and in my business.' Fifteen years on, her business is doing very well. The business's success no doubt gives them a sense of being on the right track, no matter how difficult it felt early on.

She sighs: 'We've gone through some real ups and downs. Sometimes I wonder if he stays with me now because the money is good and he is dependent on me. I notice it in that he will often be absolutely lovely to me right before he asks for something! I find that a bit depressing. Before, if he wanted something, he'd just be aggressive and say 'I'm going to do this!' Now he still tells me, but after he's been particularly sweet to me for a few days.'

GENDER ROLES IN A GLOBAL VILLAGE

Some couples decide to follow *her* high potential career path wherever it takes *them*.

Pamela, who is English, and Sebastian, an American, have been married just four years. While they met in California, they decided to move to the UK. They were pragmatic, knowing they should move wherever her job prospects in the energy sector were stronger. Sebastian faced difficulty getting a work visa and arrived in the UK just as the recession hit, limiting his potential work in the construction industry.

Since his arrival, Pamela has been the main breadwinner. Excluding a few pieces of contract work in construction, Sebastian has become a stay-at-home dad to their young daughter, Alexa. Pamela says: 'I think he's mostly okay with the fact that I'm the earner for us all. He's frustrated because he had good contacts in California, and it takes time to build up a reputation in a new place.'

She adds: 'Sebastian's great with our daughter, and she only goes to nursery two afternoons a week. They are a real pair. He's six foot two and in his early fifties. Alexa's just two and turning into a real daddy's girl. When she first came home from the hospital, he'd nervously ask: 'Am I holding her the right way?' Now, he knows her daily routines much better than I do.'

Pamela would be happy if Sebastian stopped looking for construction work and made day care of Alexa his main contribution to the family. But when I ask her about the likelihood of him doing so, she says quickly: 'Zero! I know he likes to work and that is a big part of how he defines himself. He does get some satisfaction out of it. I also know he loves being with Alexa, and he recognises how expensive day care is, so he knows he's contributing.'

Pamela is being scrupulously honest, in pointing out the financial and not just psychological value of Sebastian's contributions. Childcare costs in the UK are rising at a rate that is double inflation, which means most families feel the pinch.[63]

Childcare costs outstripping inflation is an issue in other

---

[63] Childcare Costs Annual Survey (2010) DayCare Trust, www.daycaretrust.org.uk

developed countries as well. What are the benefits to being the main breadwinner? She says: 'This is going to sound dreadful since I am married, but I love the sense of independence. I have always been able to take care of myself. That's even more important now that I have Alexa. I know I could always take care of us.'

The downside is that she now feels a stronger sense of responsibility. She remembers: 'If I hadn't married Sebastian, I probably would have continued pottering and taking temporary contracts around the world. But this pushed me into taking my future, *our* future, much more seriously. One of us had to have a more reliable source of income. I was made redundant soon after she was born. In the past I would've used the payout on another gap year. This time I thought, *I can't afford to blow this money.*'

THE RISE OF THE EXPATRIATE WOMAN

As women take on more senior roles, they are being offered greater opportunities to travel for work and even relocate as part of a promotion. Many couples begin to realise that in new and exotic locations, having him at home makes a relocation easier for the whole family, and her more likely to succeed in her new role.

Anita and Jacques met as students and have been married for fourteen years. Anita is Welsh and Jacques is French. The couple have lived with their four sons in a variety of countries in Europe and South America. They were historically on a par in earnings, but a move to Germany for a good job five years ago meant Anita began to earn significantly more than Jacques. She says: 'When I got a great sales job in Frankfurt, we decided Jacques would stay home to help us all settle in to yet another international move.'

Many couples assume that the right time for a parent to stay at home is when a child is first born. Interestingly, this couple made the decision that Jacques would stay at home when their youngest son was three and their oldest was nine. Jacques has now been at home more or less full-time for five years.

Anita reflects: 'I know how useful it is for boys to have their dad around, so that was also a small consideration. But it was the move itself that made the decision for us. Setting up a new bilingual home and settling children into a foreign language school just became too difficult with us both working. I was earning okay, but money wasn't the main trigger that suddenly freed up Jacques. We had a finely honed programme to manage our jobs and the diaries of four boys, but if anything got thrown off kilter, it was too difficult.'

Anita made steady progress in her sales job. She remembers: 'Jacques is so good on the home front; I probably abused the situation a bit. I became the man I didn't want to marry; I'd travel a lot, come home, put my feet on the table and a well-balanced dinner would be there ready for me! For the first few years, I'd say yes to every job request, and never ask Jacques if that was okay.'

Anita elaborates on the challenges of being an expatriate family: 'The process of being an expat worker is just not set up for a family without someone at home handling everything. The whole model is built on having a woman at home. I would not have been able to do my job without Jacques.' The system is built on the expectation that behind every good man is a better woman.

As Anita and so many of the other women's stories illustrate, companies that make international placements have to adjust to the idea that the supporting partner might be a man, *if* there is any support at all. This assumption still causes major problems for dual-earner couples and single employees who struggle to acclimatise, and who feel isolated in a new culture.

After the first year of being an at-home dad, Jacques played golf and got his motorbike licence, but he missed social interaction with adults. He tried a few short-term interim roles. Ultimately this was unfulfilling and the nanny they hired cost as much as what he was bringing home. Anita smiles: 'We'd had nannies when they were little, but by this time the boys were spoiled by having their dad around, and no one else would do.'

Jacques gave up work a second time to return to being a stay-at-home father, a role in which he clearly excels. Anita says: 'I often step back and observe them, seeing the boys interact with each other and with Jacques. The house could run perfectly well without me. Jacques does all the cooking, cleaning, books the most extraordinarily well-organised holidays. He knows that I can always bring in more money than him so he just lets me get on with it.'

She continues: 'The only time it ever bothered me was when things weren't going well for me at work. I wasn't getting the recognition I needed and was having real problems with a few of my colleagues. If I had lost my job at that point, I would have completely despaired. I felt a bit of jealousy towards what Jacques has with the boys.' Credit and recognition for our contributions, whether they be in the home or workplace, are vital to feeling happy in either sphere.

Anita says: 'The hardest thing is when Jacques complains on a bad day, because the boys haven't done their homework or they give him a hard time over baths. You don't often get much gratitude at work, but you get even less from children. I sometimes resent his complaints and retort that I'd love to be at home. Actually, I don't think I could handle it! Jacques's male friends also say they are jealous because it looks like an easy set-up for him, but none of them would dare to do it themselves.'

Redundancies for men, paired with
a woman who can be a main earner,
create new options.

•

A sense of choice is vital for at-home dads.

•

Success as an expatriate relies on
at-home support.

4

HOW WAS IT FOR HER? THE FEMALE EXPERIENCE OF BREADWINNING

*'My idea of superwoman is someone who
scrubs her own floors.'*

BETTE MIDLER

It is not a coincidence that since women have joined the workforce in greater numbers, western societies have enjoyed healthier economies and an improved standard of living. Increasing the participation of women in the workforce is a key factor to improving global economies and reducing poverty. Populations are only operating at half capacity if 50 per cent of their citizens are neither educated nor working for pay.

You cannot talk about primary breadwinning women without talking about their children, and what it means to be a working mother who is also the main earner. These mothers are not just providing for themselves and their partners, but very often for an entire family.

Historically, people have debated whether mothers should work outside the home at all. Given the high numbers of mothers not only working, but earning a significant amount of the family income, continuing this debate is a moot point.

By the summer of 2009, women made up half of all workers

on US payrolls, up significantly from 35 per cent in 1969.[64] Many people believe that women in these roles play a secondary role in their children's lives. This idea is born out of assumptions around fathers who historically worked late while their stay-at-home wives handled all aspects of childcare. What I found in my research couldn't be more different.

Most primary breadwinning wives went home to do a 'double duty' of domestic work as well. This may not have been all the household chores, but many said that they contributed to cooking, cleaning and childcare. This certainly fits the image painted by other research, suggesting that most breadwinning women are not entering domestic bliss when they cross the door at night.

The women I interviewed all made a special effort to be available for their children in the fewer hours they actually had with them. Indeed, only one woman out of dozens I interviewed lived away from her family during the week before coming home at weekends.

THE MYTH OF 'OPTING OUT'

It is a myth that highly trained women quit work when they have children. For example, only 16 per cent of professional American women anticipate becoming stay-at-home mothers.[65] The Centre for Work-Life Policy found that 93% of women want to return to employment after having children, though only 73% actually do, and of those only 40% are able to return to full-time, mainstream jobs[66] with a further 9% choosing self-employment. Those who 'opt-out' are not doing so because the pull of family is so great. Rather they are dismayed by the poor quality flexible options that welcome them upon their return.

---

[64] US Bureau of Labor Statistics, July 2009

[65] Stone, P & Lovejoy, M (2004) 'Fast-track women and the "choice" to stay at home', *The Annals of the American Academy of Political and Social Science*, 596, 62–83

[66] Hewlett, SA (2007) *Off-Ramps and On-Ramps: Keeping Talented Women on the Road to Success*, Harvard Business School Press

Nearly all the women I spent time with were happy that they had continued working after the birth of their children. In the US, four in ten mothers are primary breadwinners, bringing home the majority of the family's earnings, and nearly two-thirds (63 per cent) are co-breadwinners, bringing home at least a quarter of the family's earnings.[67]

The divide between home and work time is a precarious balance for most female professionals. The women I coach love their families, but they love the satisfaction of working outside the home too.

The media has a preoccupation with 'work-life balance', which often plays upon the underlying fears of women who work outside the home. They worry that they are spending less time with their children than their mothers did with them. This is simply not true. Women are very adept at protecting the time they have for their children, even while spending longer on the job.

In fact, between 1985 and 2000, mothers spent an average of four more hours at the paid job per week and five more hours parenting.[68] Women are spending less time on housework, volunteering and on *themselves*. Children have not suffered in terms of total hours, but the working mothers have in terms of less free time, less sleep and less socialising. Technology is the best and worst thing to happen to working women; the flexibility it offers also means the work 'day' gets stretched into the evenings and weekends.

Katrina, a mother of three, is a good example of this. She remarked several times that she felt she was a better mother because she was working. She explains: 'I value the little time I have with them. I get excited when I get to pick them up from school. I remember being in a queue of mothers picking up their kids a few years ago. Kids were climbing into their SUVs and their mothers driving away talking on their mobile phones and it hit me, "Oh my gosh, they don't realise how lucky they are, they

---

[67] US Census Bureau, Bureau of Labor Statistics, Current Population Survey 2009
[68] Bianchi, S, Robinson, J, Milkie, M (2006) 'Changing Rhythms of American Family Life', Russell Sage Foundation

get to do this *every* day!" I treasure every minute with the kids because I don't have the *luxury* of every minute with the kids.'

Katrina routinely gets to work at 6:30am. In fact, our interview was scheduled for 7am, the only time she had free that week. She continues: 'It's one of the reasons I get to work so early. If I leave when they are sleeping there's a chance I can get home earlier in the afternoon. I don't read for fun any more, I don't socialise and I don't exercise. Any spare time I have goes to the kids.'

Sighing, she continues: 'I hope my kids will never say I wasn't there. I want to be able to say I did a decent job as a mom and a wife *and* as a worker. I'm doing my damnedest to make sure there will be no regrets. I had a young colleague from Tokyo come into my office this week. She wants to start a family but wondered how she could combine career and family. I said, "Look around my office at all the family photos. You can totally do it. I know you will be a better mom for it." I also want to show my daughter that you can have work you love and a family.'

When asked more about the impact she felt her work had on her nine-year-old daughter, Fanny, she says: 'She's a spitfire and I could see her running this company someday. Right now she says she wants to be a nanny when she grows up. While some moms might be resentful that she has such a great relationship with her nanny, I actually find it reassuring. It's evidence that we chose the right person to bring into our family and there is one more person in Fanny's life that loves her. Our children were involved in the weddings of our last two nannies, and they still write to ask for pictures of the kids. Simon and I know it's about the support network we build for our family that extends beyond us.'

Similarly protective about her time with her children, Barbara, a mother of two, says: 'I have two priorities: my family and my work. I have always been very clear to my employers about those boundaries. I don't do cocktail parties. I don't travel at the weekends. I want to be home to put my kids to bed at night. I'll work from home when I have to take the kids to the doctor, but I don't even remember the last time I read a book!

'I have colleagues who live much closer to work than I do, but they still say they never see their children during the week. That's not an option for me. This is a pace I have chosen for myself, and I don't believe I've ever been held back because of it. I think some women don't have enough confidence in themselves to say to their bosses, "I will give you 110 per cent while I'm here – but this is where I draw the line."'

Adam Quinton, of the Gender and Policy Program at the School of International and Public Affairs at Columbia University, says female breadwinners are 'Under a much larger amount of stress if an important meeting clashes with school sports day. While she knows the family depends on her income, maternal guilt means she feels she has to be at her child's event.

'I think men don't worry about those family responsibilities as much. His sense of contribution to the family is by attending the business meeting to keep his job, not primarily the sports day. He can go on, relatively guilt free, and achieve his career ambitions knowing that's the way he contributes to the family. It's very tough for women in this position as they often have a greater sense of overall responsibility. Not just for the job, but for their family's happiness.'

FROM WORKING WOMAN TO WORKING *MOTHER*

How much does being the primary breadwinner matter when a woman wants to have children and how much influence does it have over how many children she actually has? Surprisingly little.

What I found was that while all working women may face challenges when thinking about how to time having children, being the main earner didn't make that decision any more difficult. In my consultancy, I often 'maternity coach' women who are pregnant and about to take maternity leave.

The process involves helping her prepare for the huge mental shift of potentially going from back-to-back meetings on a Friday to having a newborn child in her arms on the Monday and the prospect of several months at home ahead of her.

Essentially we look at how she can keep her career on track and assimilate her feelings about being a working woman into being a working *mother*. I then help her to readjust to the demands of work when she eventually returns, regain confidence and a sense of career direction, and maximise opportunities. Sometimes a woman is unsure whether she even wants to return to paid work, or would rather change her schedule to part-time.

Noticeably, these conversations almost never happen if the recent mother is also the main breadwinner. There is little option but to return. Her growing family needs her income. I once was talking about this issue with a group of HR executives, and one said: 'We love female breadwinners! They never give us a hard time about when they are coming back. They are motivated because they *have to* work.'

To this end, I expected female breadwinning to have affected the way a couple plans to have a family. I was surprised that for most women, being the breadwinner did not get in the way of family plans. In some cases the woman had children prior to being the main breadwinner. However, barring problems with infertility, these women had children when they *wanted* children.

If anything, the fact that they out-earned their partners forced the conversation of whether they wanted someone to be home with the child –and if so, could it be the child's father?

> *Most families rely very much on mothers' income.*
>
> •
>
> *The vast majority of women anticipate continuing work after having children.*
>
> •
>
> *Women sacrifice free time for themselves rather than deprive kids or work.*

THE ART OF TIMING

Elise and Lionel have been married sixteen years. At the beginning of the relationship, they earned on the same scale. She worked in accountancy and he in banking. Elise is one of the few women who consciously waited until she had achieved a certain level of career success before getting pregnant. She wanted to become a partner at her architecture firm.

She explains: 'My company started out as a small partnership, and the opportunities for growth were fantastic. I earned several rapid promotions. I just knew it would be easier to leverage more freedom if I was senior.'

By the time their first daughter, Karen, was born, Elise was indeed a partner and on a higher salary than Lionel. Lionel openly told other couples that if he and Elise ever had children, he would be happy to stay at home. She says: 'Before we had children, he was always the favourite uncle to my sister's kids. I knew he would be great with our own, and he was open to the idea from the beginning.'

When Karen was born, they initially placed her in nursery. During this time, Lionel was made redundant from a job he didn't enjoy. They began to discuss what they would do for childcare if they had a second child. They could manage on one income if need be, knowing that even if Lionel got another job, it would be precarious because redundancies were common in banking.

Elise explains: 'I don't think it was a series of conscious choices we made; it just felt right. Lionel certainly deserved time off after 20 years working in the city. Lionel spent time with Karen, played golf and went out for lunch with his mates occasionally. After he'd been job-hunting for eight months, Karen's nursery closed down and we were forced to make a decision.'

She continues: 'We knew we wanted Karen to carry on with some sort of part-time day care to give us both a break. We looked at several nurseries, but the one we liked was only open between nine and three. It completely ruled out both of us working full-time. We also knew that we wanted a second child at some point. I don't remember it feeling like a hard decision for either of us.'

While it was a situation they might not have planned, Lionel's skills with the children and her career potential meant it worked better than a more traditional arrangement.

Elise's breadwinning role affected the timing of their second daughter. Her employer only gave the minimum legal maternity leave so Elise knew she would have to go back after six weeks. This transition was made much easier knowing that Lionel was at home with the girls. Elise says: 'I saw some of my friends who had part-time jobs. They always seemed pulled in two directions. Our arrangements allowed me to have peace of mind because Lionel is far better with the children than I would be. The ballet teacher thinks he's a brilliant dad. He always manages to have their hair up in perfect buns when he takes them to lessons.'

There is no masculine angst for Lionel around childcare. Elise says: 'Not surprisingly, he struggled most when they were babies. I remember it myself from my few weeks of maternity leave. I'd just crave adult stimulation!' Lionel made the most of his social network, going out for lunch when he got a chance, and has always been invited to mums' coffee mornings. He is also confident which, like some of the other men, may have helped him adapt to this non-traditional role.

Other men have commented to them both how lucky Lionel is and how they would love to be at home with their children. Elise suspects this sense of being envied has helped him feel stronger in the role. Lionel's family is similarly supportive. Several years ago his brother built a business, sold it and no longer works for pay. Elise laughs: 'We joke with his parents at Christmas how they raised two strapping lads, neither of whom work!'

HOW LOUD IS HER BIOLOGICAL CLOCK?

Huge tension can arise when one person wants to start having children, and the other is not ready or willing. Needless to say, it is even harder when it is the female breadwinner who wants to take a career break to have children. Maria was one such woman.

Originally from Spain, she found work in the financial sector just a few months after arriving in the UK as a university student and setting up house with her partner, Elliott. At just 22, she took over the steady breadwinning role. Throughout his twenties, Elliott alternated between years of further education offset by occasional lucrative consultancy work creating musical scores for television and movie productions.

In their first years together, there was little difference in their individual earnings. He would undertake remunerative consultancy projects now and again, whereas she held a steady job that paid the bills on a day-to-day basis. She says: 'It was at least ten years into our relationship before I truly realised that our definitions of success were very different. I wanted the things I assumed everyone wanted: a nice house, children, a garden, a dog. I never made the connection that what attracted me to Elliott, his love of doing interesting work regardless of whether or not it earned well, would become the sticking point for us.'

Elliott's working style was also not conducive to steady employment. Maria explains: 'I remember one of his happiest times working on a particularly challenging score. He was up all hours and I would bring him coffee at three in the morning. He cracked it four weeks later, which gave him the greatest sense of achievement.'

Elliott dabbled at teaching music, but found the daily interaction with students difficult. He preferred to devote long hours at night to composing music.

The crisis came eight years into their relationship when Maria turned 30. She was now earning far more than Elliott and wanted to have children. However, Elliott showed no signs of settling into a more predictable job. She says: 'I thought we had an unspoken contract: *I work hard, you study hard and when we want a family, you will support us while I am with the children.* When we reached that point, he just didn't want that responsibility. He said quite plainly, "Maria, you know who I am." I did and it broke my heart.'

Maria may have had the contract *in her mind*, but it had never been agreed or even discussed before she felt ready to start a family. Likewise, Elliott imagined they would continue as normal, giving him the freedom to work towards that one great musical score – a goal he believed he had been clear about from the beginning.

Elliott then made a demand of his own: after earning a Master's degree in his mid-twenties, he now wanted to start a PhD. This was a decision that would prevent him from earning for at least another four years. Needless to say, this added immense pressure to the relationship.

Then, piling on further stress, just a few months after he enrolled, Maria bought their first flat and was made redundant just a month later. The flat was in her name only, as had been Elliott's request. When she asked if he could use some of the savings for his final years of study to help pay the mortgage, he refused. He reasoned that it was her decision they buy a flat rather than continue to rent, an option with which he had been happy.

She recalls: 'When he said that, it nearly broke us. It made me realise that not only could I not rely on him for the children I wanted, it was completely up to me to maintain the situation we were already in.'

Swallowing her bitterness, Maria waited those four years. However, she kept him to his word and after he graduated in June, she was pregnant by September. How did she get through all those difficult years?

She says: 'I was so angry! I hated him a lot of the time. But we had a strong relationship with lots of history. I also felt guilty for blaming him and didn't want to be unsupportive of his dream. And I was scared of raising a child by myself. My career was certainly a good distraction. Years later, I wonder if it was really Elliott's fault we didn't have children earlier. Would I really have chucked in my career if the timing had been right? Maybe not.'

Her career, whilst a vital distraction during those difficult years, was not her only motivation. She admits: 'If I had to be really honest, I wanted to have children with Elliott. I was angry with him, but I loved him too. I knew that I wanted *him* to be the father of my children. I probably also knew that if I left him at 30, it would take me several more years to find another man I loved enough to want a family with.'

Having found the ideal father for her future, she decided to wait it out. She says: 'I wasn't so clear and cynical as it perhaps sounds now. I probably also thought, *I'll wait and have the kids I want. If it doesn't work out with Elliott at least I'll have the children!* After all the good years we had together, I didn't want him to destroy my chances of having my ideal family.'

After completing his PhD, Maria says Elliott started his 'proper career', though she still significantly out-earns him. He now works for a larger firm creating music for the media, spending three days a week in the office and two at home. They have a full-time nanny.

With their first child, Maria took four months off, which she felt was too little time. After having her other children, she took six months off because she was legally protected to have exactly the same job if she returned within that period.

CHILD-FREE VERSUS CHILD-LESS

Of course, not all breadwinning wives have children. When women break through the glass ceiling, the cost is often childlessness. Fertility rates in the UK and several other European nations have fallen below the replacement rate of 2.2 children for every one woman. An increasing proportion of women are delaying having children or choosing not to have them at all. In fact, a quarter of women born in 1972 will be childless at age 45.[69]

As Sylvia Ann Hewlett wrote in her 1993 report for UNICEF: 'The hard-edged personality cultivated by many successful professionals – control, decisiveness, aggressiveness, efficiency – can be *directly at odds* with the passive, patient, selfless elements in good nurturing... Qualities needed for career success also include efficiency, a controlling attitude, an orientation towards the future and an inclination towards perfectionism, while *their virtual opposites* – tolerance for mess and disorder, an ability to let go, and appreciation for the moment and an acceptance of difference and failure – are what is needed for successful parenting.'[70]

---

[69] Office of National Statistics (2000) 'Britain 2000: The Official Yearbook of the UK'
[70] Hewlett, SA (1993) 'Child Neglect in Rich Nations', UNICEF Report

She also discusses in *Creating a Life: Professional Women and the Quest for Children* that while 42 per cent of women in senior corporate roles are childless, only 14 per cent actively choose not to have children.

The opposite is true for men. Almost half (49 per cent) of 40-year-old women executives earning $100,000 or more are childless, while only 10 per cent of 40-year-old male executives with equivalent earnings do not have children.[71] Clearly, professional men have not felt the need to choose between an executive career and having children.

Breadwinning wives without children can face the double whammy of disrespect from others. People can incorrectly assume that not only do female breadwinners without children emasculate their husbands, they are selfish and unfeeling for not being mothers. The success of these women too frequently only serves to highlight the assumptions of naysayers; the women are clearly too focused on themselves to understand the selfless act of motherhood or being a good wife.

Amelia, who works as a contractor in government offices, struggled with infertility before having her son. Her struggle was made all the harder knowing she couldn't take as much time off as she would like after his eventual birth since she was the primary breadwinner.

In the end she took six months' maternity leave, but had to save for several years beforehand to finance that time. She is a contractor, entitled to no maternity leave and only statutory pay. She says: 'We want more kids – but if we were to have another child, we'd have to save again. That affects timing and it's hard enough to conceive in the first place without worrying about how you are going to pay for the months you spend with the baby!'

---

[71] Hewlett, SA (2002) 'Creating a Life: Professional Women and the Quest for Children', Miramax

THE AGE-OLD QUESTION:
WHAT DO WOMEN WANT?

Interestingly, most female breadwinners rarely thought about their partner's earning potential when they first met. Instead, they used characteristics like 'funny', 'kind', 'laid back', 'supportive', 'attractive' and 'relaxed' to describe what they thought of the men in their lives. These word choices are interesting as they denote characteristics many high-achieving professional women wanted in their lives: someone who will help them relax and boost their spirits. They needed men who would support their successes without feeling threatened.

Rather than put the emphasis on *finding* a great provider, most women built lives where they could *be* the great provider. Looking for a partner who was psychologically supportive was vital, if not always a conscious decision for most of them. While most women perhaps did not anticipate out-earning their future husbands, they all knew they would work outside the home.

One of the first pieces of phenomenological research on the experiences of female breadwinners, conducted by Rachel Meisenbach,[72] uncovered six areas of similarity between women who are the primary breadwinners for their families:

1 Having control.

2 Valuing independence.

3 Feeling pressure and worry.

4 Valuing partner's contributions.

5 Feeling guilt and resentment.

6 Valuing career progress.

---

[72] Meisenbach, R (2010) 'The female breadwinner: Phenomenological experience and gendered identity in work/family spaces', *Sex Roles*, 62, 2–19

Independence was the most commonly mentioned benefit to being the main breadwinner. Research by Aviva that found than fewer than one in ten women (nine per cent) would like to swap places with their partner to become the stay-at-home parent,[73] and most of the women I spoke with would not wish to trade places with their husbands. They openly admitted how much they personally enjoy their jobs and their earning power.

The other side of the coin was the sense of responsibility and even resentment that can accompany the role. My own findings echoed Meisenbach's. For example, when I asked what she valued about being a primary breadwinner, Vashti, a security specialist whose husband also works full-time, was thoughtful: 'I like that I can contribute on such an equal footing. When I look at girlfriends who don't bring home much money, I'm glad I'm not in that position. They are cost-conscious and have to ask their partners for cash.'

Vashti's feelings were echoed by most of the female breadwinners I spoke to. Many of them never considered the benefits of being the main breadwinner until they looked at the experiences of friends who weren't. Vashti says: 'If Terence earned more than me next year, I would be pleased for him. I enjoy earning, but I don't feel a huge sense of responsibility. If I had to bring home 100 per cent, though, it would probably be very different.'

Her husband earns well and is very ambitious, which probably helps explain why breadwinning is not the burden for her that it is for other women. Indeed, for other women who did bring home virtually all of the bacon, the sense of responsibility was more omnipresent, though it was not disabling.

THE BUCK STOPS WITH HER

Allison reflected: 'I've never thought of myself as the breadwinner, even though I have been doing it for the last six years. It's not a role I identify with, even though that's exactly what I am. I try

---

[73] Aviva press release 'Ten Times More Stay-at-home Dads than Ten Years Ago', 7 April 2010

not to think about it because it's a lot of responsibility. I took on the financial challenge of being a contractor all those years ago, simply because I assumed George would be contributing too. Sometimes I would be working and other times he would be. There was often an overlap but now, because his business is developing so slowly, it's up to me and that's very uncomfortable.'

When asked about the downsides of being the main breadwinner, Katrina admits: 'We have lived a relatively conservative life. I know I could get another job, but there is an overwhelming sense of responsibility. I know I have to keep my head in the game. Sometimes I'd love to switch off and read a novel, but my main motivation is for the people I love. When the market was bad, I felt pressure, not so much for my own job, but for those in my team.' Katrina is loyal and very focused on providing for those around her and, like many working women, puts herself last.

Katrina works long hours on Wall Street while her husband is a full-time teacher who works shorter hours in order to be around for their three children. She says she feels no resentment that her husband gets to spend so much time with their children, but admits: 'It would probably be different if I was a clock-watcher and didn't like my job. The only time I may have felt any resentment was during a difficult merger. The office was not a fun place to be. But at the end of the day, I don't feel forced to do this. I have options, which is probably the key.'

One way Katrina, who is in her forties and routinely works fourteen-hour days, feels like she is in control is the knowledge that she could afford to retire if she wanted. She and her husband have always made saving money a priority. Living below their means meant she feels much less pressure than other breadwinners she works with, male *or* female.

THE UGLY FACE OF RESENTMENT

While the female breadwinning worked well on the whole for most couples, even the most enlightened woman could occasionally feel resentment towards her partner. Resentment is the other side of the coin of gratitude. No doubt male breadwinners can also feel resentment and pressure at times. It is relatively new for women to discuss resentment because of their earning responsibilities.

Annie is a documentary film maker. She is married to Graham, six years her junior, whom she met when he was a production assistant at the same company. She jokes: 'I didn't go looking for Graham. But when you work the kind of hours I do, you spend the most time with people from work.' This is a common issue for both men and women who work long hours. It's not surprising so many couples meet at work. At the time she was separated and about to be divorced from Jonathan, a freelance graphic designer.

Within the first few minutes of our discussion, Annie remarks that her high earnings were the main factor in her divorce from her first husband. She says: 'I learned a lot of things the hard way. I met Jonathan when we were both young. I was a straight-laced trainee documentary film maker. He was this cool, alternative artist with piercings!

'I imagine it can be hard for a guy who earns so much less and it's probably why I am easier on Graham than I was with Jonathan. You have to be a pretty confident guy to be with a woman who earns so much more. I probably wasn't as sympathetic as I could have been. By the time Jonathan and I got marriage counselling, it was far too late. I know my earnings were an issue because he once complained in a couples' therapy session, "Well, it would be helpful if every time we got in an argument, you didn't tell me to go and get a bloody job!"' She smiles knowingly: 'That's probably why I am more sensitive with Graham.'

With Jonathan, Annie was annoyed by how dedicated he was to his freelance design work. He turned down better paid and steadier work including university lecturing. To Annie, Jonathan took the moral high ground. He seemed happy to allow her to pay all the bills so he could save his time for his art.

She says: 'Eventually, every argument descended into money. Towards the end of the relationship he would lash out at anything to undermine my confidence. He gave me a hard time about my driving, something he thought he did better than me. It was a year after we were divorced before I could bear to get behind a wheel again.'

Annie still sees her first husband occasionally, and says that after they divorced he was no more motivated to find well-paying work. She explains: 'He's married to a fellow artist, and money is just not important to either of them.' This is different from the experience of several other women, whose partners became more motivated to work after they split.

In fact, Annie had to pay a one-off lump sum of alimony to Jonathan. This equated to the increase in value of their family home during the time they were together. She says she was quite surprised to find herself in her late twenties having to pay Jonathan a settlement: 'I was horrified, to be honest! I thought of our short marriage as a learning experience, and thought we would each go our own ways. My lawyer explained that in the few years we had been together, he had come to expect a certain lifestyle, which was true enough.'

Annie and her second husband, Graham, have two children under the age of ten. When I ask if Graham is involved with the children on a day-to-day basis, Annie laughs out loud, and says: 'We have a full-time nanny who does everything. He works from home, but doesn't do any school runs or cooking. I do all of that. We talked about it when considering starting a family. He was clear that he would hate to do the childcare. But then, so would I. Sometimes I think if he earned more I could go down to four days a week to be at home more, but I really love my job and I'm not sure I actually would do that even if I were given the choice.'

She continues: 'I love my weekends with them, but with the day-to-day arts and crafts stuff and music lessons for the kids, I think I would go crazy – so I understand how he feels.' Annie admits she is probably more comfortable with the primary breadwinner role simply because she is not keen to reduce her hours. She thinks she would probably resent Graham more if she were waiting for his business to become successful so that she could work less herself.

Women whose partners took over the running of the household were in the minority. Annie goes on: 'It's exhausting knowing it's all on me, but it's only on my low days that I really think about the responsibility.' As she says these words I am left with the impression that she could say this even if she earned *less* than her husband. That she is the breadwinner does not seem to be the main issue. Instead, I suspect the real issue for Annie, and for many of the other women I met, is how much day-to-day juggling they still do, whether or not their partners work at all.

This is a surprise. I had, perhaps quite naively, anticipated that men who were not working or could determine their day since they were self-employed would take up much of the slack. This was simply not the case.

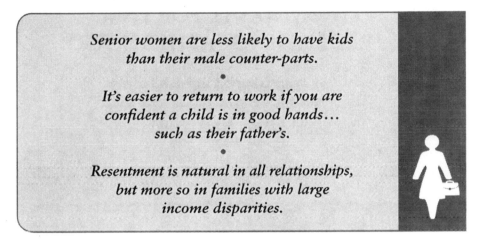

Senior women are less likely to have kids than their male counter-parts.

•

It's easier to return to work if you are confident a child is in good hands... such as their father's.

•

Resentment is natural in all relationships, but more so in families with large income disparities.

5

HOW WAS IT FOR HIM?
REDEFINING FATHERHOOD

'My heart is happy, my mind is free.
I had a father who talked with me.'

ABIGAIL VAN BUREN
Dear Abby column

You cannot talk about female breadwinners without talking about the men with whom they spend their lives. Similarly, you cannot talk about what it means to be the man in these relationships without addressing the evolving history of the stereotypical male role and what it means to be a provider and father.

Being a provider for one's family is so linked to the idea of being the 'man of the house' that, as Bill Bryson points out in *At Home: A Short History of Private Life*, 'The Head of the Household was the 'husband' – a compound term meaning literally "householder" or "house owner". His role as manager and provider was so central that the practice of land management became known as husbandry. Only much later did "husband" come to signify a marriage partner.'[74]

The concept of the 'ideal man' is open to interpretation and is historically fluid. In the US, for example, before the 1770s the perfect man was a genteel landowning patriarch living off

---

[74] Bryson, B (2010) *At Home: A Short History of Private Life*, Doubleday, p 54

the profits from his estate. By the 1800s, that had changed to a rugged individualist, who provided for his family from the toil of his hands, through farming or carpentry for example. By the twentieth century, that image had given way to the more modern ideal of a competitive breadwinner who was a self-made man, an ideal combination for success and the opportunities of an industrial society.

The meanings ascribed to this word came to define men, and the expectations placed upon them, more than we could ever imagine. The gendered expectation of male as provider is widespread. Indeed, research shows that families from Canada, Belgium[75] and the US actively construct a sense of male as breadwinner, even long after a male job loss and when the wife and even the children are technically fulfilling the breadwinning role.[76]

Certainly these expectations are still with us today. According to a 2010 report by the Pew Research Centre, 33 per cent of survey respondents feel it's important for a woman to be able to support a family before getting married, while 67 per cent say it's important for a man to be able to do so.[77]

MEN: THE NEW JUGGLERS

The conflict comes for men, as it has done for women, in balancing work and family needs.

Women, taking on a greater share of the breadwinning, are asking for more help and many men are indeed answering the call. While issues with work/life balance have historically and unhelpfully been considered a 'women's issue', men are increasingly feeling the pressure. Over a 30-year period, men's reported level of work-life conflict rose from 34 per cent as long

---

[75] Doucet, A & Merla, L (2007) 'Stay-at-home Fathering: A strategy for balancing work and home in Canadian and Belgian families', *Community, Work and Family*, 10, 453–471
[76] Buzzanell P & Turner, L (2003) 'Emotion work revealed by job loss discourse: Backgrounding-foregrounding of feelings, construction of normalcy and reinstituting of traditional masculinities' *Journal of Applied Communication Research*, 31, 27–57
[77] Pew Research Centre Publications (2010) 'The Decline of Marriage and Rise of New Families'

ago as 1977 to 45 per cent in 2008, while women's struggle with work-life only marginally increased (34 per cent to 39 per cent) during this period.[78]

In fact, the greatest amount of stress is felt by men in dual earner couples, as opposed to those where the man is the only earner. These men are recognising that, just as their women work and manage family responsibilities, so must they.

Indeed, fathers are more involved in the lives of their children than at any other time in recent history. Between 1985 and 2000, fathers were also feeling the squeeze to make the most of their time: two more hours at their job and four more hours parenting per week.[79]

A Pew Centre survey found that almost two-thirds (62 per cent) of Americans surveyed endorse the modern marriage in which the husband and wife *both* work and both take care of the household and children. This is a significant increase from fewer than half of people (48 per cent) in 1977.[80]

Needless to say, shared responsibilities require new ways of adapting. There are various ways in which working parents cope with demanding schedules. Tag-team parenting is popular among more working-class parents who are more likely to work in shifts or for an hourly wage. These parents work opposite schedules to ensure that someone is always available for the children.

While some jobs lend themselves to this type of arrangement, most professional positions do not easily fit within these types of shifts. Instead, buying in help, in the form of nursery, full-time childcare or even boarding school is popular with professionals who can afford and want this type of support.[81] The families I talked to used a variety of methods including nurseries, nannies, other family members and after-school programmes, often simultaneously, to

---

[78] Galinsky, E et al (2009) 'Times are Changing: Gender and Generation at Work and at Home', Families and Work Institute

[79] Bianchi, S, Robinson, J, Milkie, M (2006) 'Changing Rhythms of American Family Life', Russell Sage Foundation

[80] Pew Research Centre Publications (2010) 'The Decline of Marriage and Rise of New Families'

[81] Boushey, H (2008) 'Family friendly policies: Helping mothers make ends meet', *Review of Social Economy*, 66 (1)

care for their children. In some cases, juggling these led to a decision that the father would stay at home to decrease their reliance on external support.

These men are not alone. There is an increase in the number of support groups for stay-at-home dads. The website www.athomedad.org lists several hundred support groups across the US. The new reality web-based comedy show called *Stay-at-Home Dad* is popular and competes for airtime with confessional-style blogs such as *Rebel Dad* and *Dudes on Diapers*.

The US nappy manufacturer, Pampers, found that 69 per cent of fathers say they change diapers as much as their wives do.[82] The company responded by signing a US football star, Drew Bees of the New Orleans Saints, as a spokesman in an effort to target these 'new fathers'.

Still, men are not picking up as much domestic work as they think they are. Surveys routinely show a discrepancy between how much men say they are doing around the house, and how much their own wives think they are contributing.[83] Almost half (41 per cent) of the breadwinning wives surveyed by *Redbook* magazine in 2010 felt they did more than half of parenting and household chores.[84]

How is there such a discrepancy between what men and women say they do around the home? One example would be men saying they 'do laundry' because they load and unload a washing machine. Women will then point out that clothes need to be collected, folded and put away as a part of 'doing laundry'. Many women complain of household chores being 'half-done'. Still, instead of following gender scripts, many men are recognising that they need to do more. In response, couples are re-negotiating roles, to fit their individual strengths and what works best for their family.

---

[82] Stout, H (2010) 'When Roles Reverse: The Rise of the Stay-at-home Husband: Is This the New Status Symbol for Alpha Women', +MSN.com August 23, 2010
[83] Minetor, Randi (2002) *Breadwinner Wives and the Men they Marry*, New Horizon Press
[84] Goad, K (2010) 'Big earning wives, and the men who love them', *MSN Lifestyle*, September 13

FROM ALPHA MALE TO BETA DAD

Linda and Brian have been married for 24 years, and have two young children. They met at university and married as soon as they graduated. Linda has been a partner in several consultancy firms for the last 15 years, and Brian worked full-time in financial services until six years ago. During the years they both worked full-time, they shared the nursery run equally. In her interview, Linda was still frustrated by '…The constant bartering and bargaining over whose morning appointment was more important.'

She describes their exhausting routine: 'We were always rushing. Even when you left work on time to pick the kids up, you were praying they went to sleep quickly because you still had more emails to deal with afterwards.' To add insult to injury, Linda also got short shrift from some of her colleagues who described her as a 'part-time' worker.

Linda says: 'Motherhood focused me as I had a finite amount of time to work. I couldn't mess about. I was organised in my time and focused on business development for the company. I also had to delegate to colleagues much more than I would have done otherwise. Within those years, my client portfolio took off. Eventually I became the managing partner of the practice. I wanted to show people that being a mother and a partner could work.'

As the managing partner, responsibility at the office was falling increasingly on to Linda's shoulders. Brian's colleagues also commented about his shortened work hours and routinely scheduled meetings after his core hours. Linda says: 'I don't think most organisations are very tuned in to the needs of working parents, let alone fathers. There is still an expectation that the school run is the wife's job, no matter what *other* job she also does.'

Brian, although disenchanted with life in financial services, earned well and so was resigned to continuing in his role. In fact, during her second maternity leave, Linda wrote a resignation letter to her partnership, saying she wanted more time with her family. Brian was made redundant the day she was due to post her resignation.

She remembers: 'Our plan had been that one of us would stay home. I was very willing to do it, and thought I could perhaps build up a small practice locally whilst raising a family. In fact, when I qualified right out of university, I was drawn to consultancy specifically because I knew it could be flexible. Plus, Brian's job in banking couldn't be done remotely. Needless to say, his bombshell changed all of that.'

Linda went back to work, in fact, taking no real maternity leave at all with her second child. As an established partner, she had members of her team ferry paperwork back and forth so that she could work from home. Brian soon found another job, but the seeds of Linda potentially being the main breadwinner had been sown. They bought a flat in central London so Linda could be close to work. She now stays in the City Monday to Friday and goes home at the weekends.

They began to reprioritise after the July 7th bombings on the London Underground in 2005. They were both commuting from Berkshire each day, and though the disruption on the rail lines lasted for a relatively short period, it pushed their finely honed balance with nursery runs out of kilter. At the same time Brian was becoming increasingly disenchanted with seemingly continuous corporate restructurings and what it meant to 'hot-desk' in the twenty-first century.

By the time they made the decision for Brian to leave work completely in 2006, their children were at school full-time. Their decision for Brian to be the at-home dad while Linda stayed in town during the week brought immediate benefits. Linda says: 'It's the little things. Brian didn't worry if I would be home for dinner or if I was stuck on a delayed train. And I don't feel guilty about my hours and like I am rushing to keep up.'

They waited until the children were school-age. Linda continues: 'I think the timing was key. Brian was relieved that he wouldn't be with the kids all day! He loves them, but he has been able to indulge in some new hobbies like the guitar. I'll be honest, I think he finds the school holidays hard!'

Several fathers were more willing to take on the role of primary caregiver after their children were a bit older and less demanding than infants. Raising children will always be the hardest job in the world. I think perhaps fathers are just a bit more honest about what they do and don't want in the role of full-time carer.

The decision that it would be Brian who stayed at home to manage this lifestyle change was easy for them. Linda says: 'Mostly it was financial. By this point I earned double his income. But it wasn't solely money. He hated his job.' She continues: 'Brian's also very practical. He can fix things around the house and maintains our cars. He was excited by the change. His only request was that if he was going to be quitting work, he wanted the full-blown lifestyle with a big house, animals and big garden. It was all or nothing for him. He didn't want to give up his job for a life in suburbia.' Brian now maintains the family from Monday to Friday.

While the children are at school, Linda is quick to point out that Brian gets on with cooking, shopping and cleaning. When the weekend comes, she takes over spending time with the children. In fact, she has delegated an increasing amount to Brian. She says: 'I used to think he could take care of the day-to-day, but that I should organise birthday parties and holidays. Now I don't, Brian gets on with it.'

What made her think she had to take responsibility for these areas in the first place? She says: 'I thought I was letting the children down. I'm not sure I'm over it. Brian is great in that he has always encouraged me to just spend the best quality time I can with the children when I am with them.'

Almost as evidence of how much she trusts Brian, Linda says he recently was responsible for narrowing down the choice of secondary schools for their eldest son to a shortlist of two which they then decided on together. Linda laughs: 'A few years ago, I would have felt that I had to do all the research and make up the lists and visit them all. Brian did a fantastic job. It's still hard not to be so involved, but it just has to be that way. Brian tells me which events I should attend and I take his advice.'

How has delegation affected their relationship? She answers: 'Our relationship has definitely become stronger. He's a great communicator so I always feel that I'm in the loop. The only downside for Brian is that he is socially isolated because we live in a village with only twelve other houses, and he certainly doesn't get invited to mums' coffee mornings. It's made worse by the fact that he can't go out in the evenings because of the children. There are no local babysitters.'

Linda says Brian shows no resentment about being reliant on her earnings. She comments pragmatically: 'We discuss everything so it's not really an issue. He's not a "man's man" anyway, the type who would be at the pub with his mates. He takes a lot of pride in a job well done; whether that is making sure the children have a good meal in the evening or organising their after-school activities.' Brian clearly derives a good deal of pride from keeping the household ticking over Monday through Friday without any external help or 'guidance' from his wife.

Interestingly, Linda continues: 'It's only the children who sometimes play up a bit! If they want something and don't like the answer he has given them, they will retort, "Well, we should ask Mummy because she earns the money!" I think the relationship I have with my children is more like the relationships a lot of men have had with theirs. It's a real novelty when I am home at the weekend. They don't want anything to do with their dad until Monday morning which actually suits him fine too. He gets a break!'

Linda is the only breadwinning mother I met who likened her situation to that of more traditional fathers. Even so, she is clear that her weekend time is dedicated to the children because she is the only woman who lives away during the week, rather than arising from any abdication of responsibility or remoteness from her children.

DEVALUING FATHERHOOD

Clearly, we are poised to re-frame fatherhood and what it means to be a supportive man in the twenty-first century. Let's make sure we do not get in our own way and devalue fathers as we have done in the past.

Indeed, fathers have a long history of being very active in the lives of their children. Historically, steady work for men was seasonal and unreliable or subject to an employer's whim. Many fathers taught their children through apprenticeships in the family trade or as future farmers or family landowners. As we moved into an industrial society, with home and workplace increasingly separated, men began to spend more time away from the family, leading to their disenfranchisement.

As the nineteenth century progressed, fatherhood was steadily de-skilled, and mothers gradually took over the day-to-day functions which had once bound fathers and children together.[85] In the twenty-first century, the First and Second World Wars stripped generations of children of a father figure. Indeed, of the survivors, many had spent so much time away from their young children that there was still a sense of remoteness when they returned, which contributed to their secondary status within the family.[86]

Allison Holland is a management consultant whose husband watches their infant son two days a week. She explains: 'He doesn't mind that I earn more money than he does, but he does mind if he is not working. He rationally recognises that he is contributing day care but he jokes about himself being a "good house husband". I know from the way he jokes that he doesn't consider it a real contribution.'

She continues: 'George sees it as a demeaning task even though he actually enjoys the two days a week he has Alexander.' Needless to say, Allison finds George's complaints about his role frustrating, particularly when he is so good with his son – and as we discussed earlier, she would love to have that time with Alexander.

---

[85] Burgess, A (1997) *Fatherhood Reclaimed: The Making of the Modern Father*, Vermilion, p 16
[86] Turner, B & Rennell, T (1995) *When Daddy Came Home: How Family Life Changed Forever in 1945*, Hutchinson

> *Modern men want to be more hands-on than their fathers were with them.*
>
> •
>
> *Support groups for at-home dads are at an all-time high.*
>
> •
>
> *The new 'ideal man' is egalitarian and very attractive to high-achieving women.*

MUMS DISEMPOWERING DADS

I think a dirty secret of mothering is that women have contributed to the disenfranchisement of fathers, as a means of legitimising their own power within the family. Historically, because they were denied so many other roles in the workplace, mothers became invested in the attitude that there was no stronger bond than between a mother and child.

We see this in the demonisation of the rare women who harm their children. It is deemed *unnatural* in a much more vehement way than how we judge abusive fathers. Now that women have greater opportunities to join the workforce and design an identity for themselves, this distancing of men from fatherhood is an artefact that must be eradicated to enable men to take on fatherhood fully.

We see this isolation from competent fatherhood portrayed in the media. They are seen in one of two stereotypical ways. In the first, Dad is a well-meaning buffoon whose heart is in the right place, but he seems happily clueless without the watchful eye of his wife. The alternative image is of the authoritarian and even abusive father who is emotionally or physically absent.

These images have reinforced the idea that only a mother can provide the right support for her children – which simultaneously alienates fathers and increases the pressure on women to be *perfect mothers*. This is particularly tricky for female breadwinners who often spend more time away from their children than they would like.

Interestingly this theme is echoed by several of the female breadwinners I met. Maureen, whose husband stays at home with their daughter, smiles: 'Next week is half term and I am sure he has not given a single thought to where Sarah is going to be during the day. If I asked him to, he probably would organise something.'

Maureen is not complaining too bitterly, however, as she continues: 'Having said that, I'm not sure I'd *want* him to take it on. Planning her school breaks validates my role as her mother. It helps me feel I'm still a good mum.'

This was true for other mothers I spoke with as well. The added responsibilities of childcare were often a reminder to *themselves* that they were still needed, no matter how capable the father of their children might be.

Carly, a research scientist, says: 'We talked about Luke watching the children. We thought he'd get another job quickly, but it dragged out over eighteen months. I don't think he would be cut out for a Mister Mom role.' Interestingly, Carly adds: 'There is probably also a part of me that feels I should be at home, and that having to do so much for the children reminds me I am needed.'

There is an element of women thinking, *I'd like more help, but I wouldn't want him to be too good at it!*

As explained by Adrienne Burgess in the groundbreaking book, *Fatherhood Reclaimed*: 'The old-style feminist argument seems to be that "we've invited men in" (to fatherhood) and they "haven't been interested". This attitude ignores the enormous cultural and structural barriers to men's participation in family life. For men to become close to their children, these barriers will have to be taken as seriously and tackled as consciously as the dismantling of barriers to women's participation in the wider world.'[87]

When men are willing to step up to these roles, breadwinning mothers must get out of their way.

---

[87] Burgess, A (1997) *Fatherhood Reclaimed: The Making of the Modern Father*, Vermilion, p 31

RECLAIMING FATHERHOOD

The rise of women's status and pay in the workplace has enabled men to take a greater role in the family, as they are increasingly relieved of the sole burden of breadwinning.

Obviously, it is not just the media and women who are being challenged by redefining the role of father. Men are facing the challenge, and indeed, thinking about it increasingly even before they become fathers. While there may be confusion as to what fatherhood means in the twenty-first century, increasingly young men are excited to take on the role.

Helen Fisher, an anthropologist from Rutgers University, conducted a study of over 5,000 single Americans for the website www.match.com. She found the stereotype of the broody female to have been turned on its head.

Half (51 per cent) of men aged 21-34 wanted children compared to 46 per cent of women the same age. The difference becomes even more pronounced as singles age, with just 16 per cent of single women between the ages of 35 and 44 wanting children compared to 27 per cent of their male contemporaries.[88]

Needless to say, these figures may be artificially high coming from a dating website where men will be seeking to attract women. However, it is interesting that men recognise the draw of potential family life.

Clearly, men are showing rapid change in how they define their roles. If you ask men abstractly what fathers are for, they may produce traditional ideas such as providing, protecting and advising. But if you ask them to outline their value to their *own* children, such functions, if mentioned at all, will be towards the bottom of the list. Instead, fathers today prioritise intimacy, tenderness and trust much more highly than the more stereotypical characteristics mentioned previously.[89]

As observed by anthropologist Margaret Mead: 'No developing

---

[88] Fisher, H (2011) 'Single in America', www.match.com
[89] Burgess, A (1997) *Fatherhood Reclaimed: The Making of the Modern Father*, Vermilion, p 32

society that needs men to leave home and do their thing for society ever allows young men in to handle or touch their newborns, for they know somewhere if they did the new fathers would become so hooked they would never go out and do their thing properly.'[90]

Another anthropologist, Carol Ember, studied Luo tribes in Kenya where boys regularly undertake domestic work alongside girls. She found that, as boys carried out more of this work, they became less aggressive and more socially skilled.[91] Certainly many of the female breadwinners talked about how their husbands had grown into and grown from a greater share of the domestic roles. They reported it made their partners more empathetic to both their children and to them as women.

Men's roles are certainly shifting and this could be a new type of benefit to women and families everywhere.

When Adrienne Burgess, director of the Fatherhood Institute, looked at the history of fatherhood in her book, *Fatherhood Reclaimed*, she found: 'The fear has not been that men, once they became close to children as women have routinely been, would find the experience unappealing. Rather the fear has been that, once accustomed to it, they would not willingly give it up.

'Men have been urged to keep an emotional and physical distance from infants so that they will be cut off from their most tender feelings, so that they will be alienated from themselves. This has helped to condition them to blind obedience, has fitted them to undertake exhausting and degrading physical work, and has prepared them to be an army in waiting in times of peace and to kill and be killed in times of war. It is surely no coincidence that only when violence is seen as anti-social, and it is unlikely that young men in large numbers will ever again be called upon to fight for our country, a review of the father's role in society is deemed possible.'[92]

However, accepting childcare as a key responsibility is not

---

[90] Quoted in Giveans, DL & Robinson, MK (1985) 'Roles Throughout the Life Cycle' in Hanson SM & Bozett (eds) *Dimensions in Fatherhood*, Sage

[91] Ember, C & Ember, M (1999) *Anthropology* 9th edition, Prentice-Hall

[92] Burgess, A (1997) *Fatherhood Reclaimed: The Making of the Modern Father*, Vermilion, p 15

straightforward for all men. In *Breadwinning Wives and the Men they Marry*, Randi Minetor found that of the dozens of men interviewed: '...The men who were most comfortable with their wives' breadwinning roles were most likely to be more involved in childcare. The rise of women's status and pay in the workplace has enabled more men to take on a greater role in the family, as they are increasingly relieved of the sole burden of breadwinning.'

In her research, Minetor found men who expressed ambivalence, discomfort, or even unhappiness with the arrangement were more likely to find childcare emasculating and stay out of it altogether. Even though they live in non-traditional relationships, with their wives carrying the breadwinning load, those husbands tend to see child-raising in the most traditional terms: women's work.[93]

I also found that women who said their husbands were most supportive of their breadwinning were those who were more hands-on with childcare. In order to accommodate family life, Simon, the husband of Katrina, gave up a lucrative job in sales to become a high school teacher.

She remembers: 'The first year after he started, I suggested we look for a beach house since he now had summers off. My kids are blessed; they spend the whole summer with their dad at the beach every year. And I am thrilled for them. Some girlfriends, who are also main breadwinners, look at our arrangement with resentment and think it is odd. "It's working out well for him!" they say. But they have to get over it. Just because I make more money doesn't make me the most important person in the house. I'm not.'

When asked what first drew her to Simon, she sighs and pauses: 'He is just a good person through and through. He's always a glass-half-full guy. We knew he could make the most difference to kids' lives at the high school level. Initially he was envious of the career networking I do. Ironically, in his role as teacher and sports coach, his network is far bigger now than it ever was when he worked in corporate life. It just looks different from how he

---

[93] Minetor, Randi (2002) *Breadwinner Wives and the Men they Marry*, New Horizon Press, p 159–161

envisioned, and since it centres on our family, it's actually more important too.'

Some of Katrina's satisfaction with the arrangement could be attributed to the fact that their lifestyle decision was a very conscious one for both of them. They did not drift into it. Problems can arise when couples 'fall into' these non-traditional roles but don't discuss it openly or even look at the potential benefits for the family. Feeling like you have a choice over the set-up is vital.

When asked how this equality breaks down in the day-to-day, Katrina says: 'At the weekend, Simon doesn't cook because it's the only time I have for cooking during the whole week. In some ways, we revert to traditional roles. He will also take the kids to mini-golf so I can sleep in. This may sound a bit "apple pie-ish" but we don't keep score. We don't say, "You got to play basketball this week, so I am going out for lunch with my friends."

'Some people take the approach that childcare is a burden. We try to free up time for each other. If one of us wants time to do something, the other looks for a way to make it happen.'

This was a fundamental in the happiest couples: a sense that they approach the relationship looking for ways to give to their partners rather than receive.

Mothers have historically undermined fathers' power to bolster their own.

•

Delegate and let him get on with it.

•

Time with children and on domestic duties enhances men's social skills.

DOT.COM DAD:
MEN AND ENTREPRENEURSHIP

I had a coaching client, Miranda, whose husband was setting up his own sound production studio. She assumed that as soon as it was financially feasible, she could cut down her full-time hours to four days a week. They invested in full-time day care and an office space so her husband could work, but the business was slow to grow. Miranda lamented that he seemed to have endless rounds of 'lunches and meetings that never led anywhere'.

After two years with no sign of progress, Miranda initiated a conversation about a 'statute of limitations'. They talked about their income and decided either the studio was profitable in six months or he would have to go back to recording work as a full-time employee. He was initially disgruntled, but responded by working harder and the studio began to break even after the four-month mark. She says: 'I'd like to think he was already just about to turn it around, but I'm not sure what would have happened if I hadn't laid my cards on the table.'

Several of the women I interviewed were married to men who were setting up businesses. With goals that the businesses would be successful, the women often hoped they wouldn't have to work so hard in the long run. It often left the unspoken question: 'How long do we wait to see if this business is sustainable?' Not addressing this question could lead to problems and resentment in the long term.

Barbara is living through a similar experience. She is an English woman who works in New York for a private bank. She and her husband, Heinrich, have two children under nine. Heinrich is Austrian and came from a prominent aristocratic background whose family lost their wealth in World War Two.

When they met, Barbara had an established career in finance. Heinrich worked at a variety of jobs in the legal sector, recruitment and banking, but none of these worked out. She wryly says: 'He was only ever interested in Africa, where his family had spent time. Hats off to him that he's decided to follow his dream, but he hasn't kept up his end of the bargain.'

Soon after they married, Heinrich decided he wanted to pursue his passion by organising adventure holidays for private clients in southern Africa. Barbara, who is thirteen years older than Heinrich, mentored him at the beginning of his business. She invested heavily, both financially and psychologically, in the business. Heinrich now spends five consecutive months of every year away from the family, hosting trips for paying clients.

Barbara says: 'If 20 years ago someone told me I'd still be working this hard at this point in my career, I would have said they were crazy.' There was an expectation that as Heinrich's business developed, she could scale back to have more time for family and her charitable work. Twelve years on this has still not happened.

She says: 'He is never going to earn the kind of money I earn in banking – but that was never the expectation. I just wanted him to become profitable, which he isn't. The trips are more like glorified long holidays. If he made the most of his downtime, which is actually most of his year, selling travel packages, networking with potential clients, doing the back office stuff, he could have made so much more of it. He is very good at being a guide and the business does take in paying clients. Overall, though, it runs at a loss and he certainly can't contribute to the running of the household.'

What does Heinrich do when he is back in the US? Barbara says: 'I honestly don't know how he spends his days.' The family has employed a full-time nanny since their first daughter was born. She does almost all aspects of daily childcare responsibilities. They also have a part-time cleaner. Certainly, his being away five months of each year is not conducive to childcare, but Barbara's disappointment stems more from his reluctance to help even when he is in the States.

She says dryly: 'He's always been completely clear that he doesn't want to look after our children, so I am still left with a $4,000 bill every month for our nanny. Don't get me wrong. The kids absolutely adore him, but he doesn't see taking care of them on a day-to-day basis as being his responsibility.'

Essentially, the couple now lead separate lives even when he is at home. Barbara and Heinrich even take separate holidays with their children, except for when they visit his family. There is a sense of resignation when Barbara describes the marriage: 'I don't know that a marriage can survive this type of pressure. I don't think he particularly feels threatened or that his esteem suffers, because he is doing what he loves. I have enabled that, and without a great deal of support in return.'

She adds: 'When you are first in love, you don't tend to have the tough talks about "if the business doesn't work, what will you do?" We never talked about how long we would wait and if it's not profitable what happens then. I never asked, "Would you be willing to look after the children?" because I hoped I wouldn't have to ask. They are *his* children too.'

When asked what advice Barbara would offer to other women breadwinners, she gives her longest pause of the interview before answering: 'It sounds terrible but you have to think about a worst-case scenario for the future. Figuring out who you are and what you want is vital. Don't overestimate the financial and time demands of children because it's always much more than anyone ever anticipates. What kind of man do you need in your life? Are you willing to be with someone who may provide for you financially, but is emotionally distant – or vice versa?'

Barbara elaborates: 'Sometimes I feel like the great imposter. I never set out to be this high flyer. My responsibilities have forced me to grow in my career. I'm on autopilot most of the time. Besides my children, I don't know what drives me.' She wryly smiles: 'Many people describe me as a *career woman* but what does that mean? I have a career *and* I'm a woman? I like what I do, but I'm not sure it's my life's ambition. I know I do a good job here. Part of that is probably motivated from the feeling that I *have* to do a good job; there is no safety net.'

What has been the impact on Heinrich? She says: 'It's not good for anyone, especially a man, to be completely reliant on their partner for everything. It ultimately undermines their self-worth and confidence. Heinrich can get stubborn and nasty, and that is born out of how his life has panned out. He might have been happier with a woman who was more reliant on him.'

Barbara and Heinrich rarely talk about these issues or the way the marriage has broken down. She says: 'We are past the point of talking. I don't have a lot of respect for him since I see how unhappy he is but he's failed to do anything about the situation. In the early days, I gave help around PR and made introductions. There's only so much you can do for someone who doesn't want your help. He digs his heels in at my suggestions now.'

Barbara talked about the early days of the relationship and how things might have been different: 'Heinrich liked my independence and he certainly was used to strong female figures; his mother worked. I think there are men who can cope with having a high-earning wife. Those men are confident in their own abilities. He's never admitted it to me, but I know he can't think of himself as a good provider. He's never going to contribute to a school bill, he can't even pay to take them to visit his parents abroad. Instead we go together because I have a problem with sending the children abroad with a man who doesn't have money in his own bank account.'

Barbara commutes two hours each way to work. Her priorities clearly revolve around giving her children the most idyllic countryside lifestyle she can. She sacrifices a good deal of personal time and happiness to do so. She said: 'I think I went beyond the point of no return with Heinrich and now we are on a treadmill. Our children are in a very good fee-paying private school and in a home they love.'

Divorce is a change Barbara is not willing to make while the children are young. She sighs: 'We could change our lives, but it would also mean changing theirs.' Barbara is clear that the marriage cannot be salvaged. She is resigned to the fact that Heinrich will not make a go of his business *nor* of being a stay-at-home father.

Like Barbara, some of the women I interviewed had not consciously chosen to be successful in a given professional field, but were confident they would be successful *whatever* they did for a living. They identified themselves as adaptable, hard-working and savvy. Rather, it was their partner who had a *passion* for a particular field or type of work. It was only later in their careers that these women started to question their own motivations. They had spent so long enabling another person's passion without figuring out what they themselves loved to do. The question 'what about me?' was left hanging in the air.

It's smart to clarify your roles and expectations. Given that female breadwinners lack role models, you may have to improvise. Discuss your expectations for expenditure and listen to his. Do you expect him to pick up his share of the saving after he finishes grad school? How long is he going to be writing his novel? What are the boundaries that will show support whilst also setting expectations?

AN UNHEALTHY SENSE OF COMPETITION

While many women said that being the main breadwinner worked well for both them and their partner, there were those who recognised that it had stirred multiple emotions in their husbands. We have already looked at the resentment women sometimes feel from the responsibility that can come with being a primary breadwinner. Now we look at couples where men felt resentment towards what they perceived as their secondary status.

Josephine, a breadwinning woman based in Paris, agreed with my suggestion that the qualities that draw a couple to each other are those that can be most difficult later. She says: 'I know Pierre loved that I was so ambitious when we met.' She smiles: 'That was okay when I was still in IT training. Now I'm sure he'd like to put the brakes on me a bit'.

Pierre works one day a week from home. He prepares the girls for school and cooks most dinners. A nanny does the school run. Josephine consults with Pierre on every potential job change as she knows it means longer hours initially. The family relies heavily on his flexibility. She doesn't take it for granted that he will always be able to take on those responsibilities.

The couple have been married for over a decade. During that time there was a short period when Pierre out-earned Josephine on a lucrative six-month contract. She explains: 'He often mentions going back to contract work after I've had a win at work or a promotion. I am being headhunted at the moment. A day or two after I told him, he casually mentioned returning to contract work. I wouldn't mind, but he only ever says these things when I am on the cusp of a new opportunity myself. I know a job change for him is not motivated by a new title or challenge. It's about earning yet more money. He wants to catch up.'

The timing of his comments does seem to be evidence of subconscious competition between the couple, and a not-so-subtle reminder to her of what Pierre feels he sacrifices for her career progress. Indeed, the threat of comparison must be great, as they started in literally the same job within the same company and have ended up in very different places. I notice that, in the couples I met who started in the same industry, the probability of competition and resentment was higher than in other couples, probably because the comparisons on career success are so easy to make.

Josephine explains: 'We usually worked on a pattern that after I made a career switch, then he could do the same. Only this time, this job opportunity came unexpectedly. I think he's a bit sore about the fact that this year was going to be "his turn". In an ideal world, I would sit tight while he is looking. We want to avoid both changing jobs at the same time. It's just too stressful otherwise.'

If they do indeed have a pattern of taking turns, Pierre's resentment could be understandable. On the other hand, Josephine is frustrated that Pierre's interest in moving jobs only ever comes when she is experiencing career advancement or indeed already being headhunted.

Her rapid progress obviously reminds him of what he thinks he is forgoing. She is clear, however, that if he didn't want her to take a certain role, she wouldn't. She adds: 'I'd listen to him, but I would probably resent it.' This sounds like the way Pierre negotiates her success: mostly encouraging, not getting in the way, but with a hint of competitiveness and potential resentment.

*Female breadwinners with male
entrepreneurs must have a strong stomach
and patience.*

•

*Set boundaries and expectations early on to
avoid problems later.*

•

*Competition can breed resentment. Focus
on what he brings to the family.*

WHEN DECIDING WHO WILL BE THE BREADWINNER, PERSONALITY BEATS GENDER

Many women looked at the decision on whose career should be in the forefront and who should stay at home as a decision based on personality, not gender. They would make comments like 'my husband is so much more suited to being with the children' or 'he's not nearly as ambitious as me' or 'he just has much more patience with the children'. These families made their decision based on inherent skills and characteristics rather than prescriptive gender roles.

Maggie and Roger fit into this category. Maggie, a physics professor, met Roger while they were students at university in Ireland. They have been married over 30 years and have three adult children. After they married, Maggie stayed in academia and Roger began teaching. By the time they had their first child, Roger was an assistant headteacher. While they were earning the same at that point, Maggie says income was never the main factor in deciding who would stay at home with their children.

She explains their logic: 'Straight after my PhD I was awarded a senior research fellowship. They are very hard to come by, but they get you straight onto the ladder. Roger was much more relaxed and not nearly as career-driven. Even announcing my pregnancy to my lab colleagues was a big deal. People who telephoned the department often assumed I must be the secretary. At conferences, when people met me they were often shocked I was so young *and* a woman. There just weren't many of us in the sciences at that time.'

She says: 'It was in the late seventies when Roger left teaching to take care of our newborn. We certainly got a mixed reaction from people. There weren't many men doing the same. To people who don't know him, Roger can come across as an alpha male. He's good with his hands and takes the lead, but in many ways he's not a regular "alpha". Some people thought I must be a bully to make my husband give up his job. Others asked, "How will he cope? Can he change nappies?" And I thought, *I hope so; he's going to be surrounded by them!*'

On reflection, Maggie thinks Roger was better suited to taking care of their children. She reflects: 'He's always been happy with his own company. If I'd been home with children, I'd have found the lack of adult interaction very difficult. But from a social point of view, I do think the stay-at-home role is much easier for women. There is already a social network of other women in the same situation. It's much harder for a man to walk into that setting. In fact, many of our close family friends are women *I* met during my weekly Mums and Tots class, rather than anyone he met during the other four days a week!'

She observes: 'There's almost a reverse discrimination that goes on. He didn't have the social network, but I also don't think he needed it as much. He's not terribly outgoing, so he didn't miss the interaction anyway.' It is this realisation of how hard the role of stay-at-home caregiver can be that makes many of the women I interviewed so grateful for the support they do get from their partners. This is particularly true for men who engage in full-time childcare.

If a woman's partner willingly takes on raising the children, arguably the toughest job in the world, and thrives in the role, the women *know* what a gift they are getting and do not take it for granted. Almost as an illustration, Maggie recalls an evening when she and a male colleague worked late at the lab to meet a deadline. She called Roger to say she would be late home. To build rapport, she turned to her colleague who had children the same age and asked if he ever felt guilty about the long hours he spent away from his family. She laughs: 'He looked at me quizzically and said, "It never even enters my mind."'

When the family moved to Ireland from England for her career, the children were finally in school which freed up Roger's time. He began to restore furniture and built up his renovation skills. He is now a self-employed builder, working on projects that interest him. They live in a rural location which suits them both. She says: 'Anyway, Roger's happiest out with our sheep and doing bits on the house.'

Maggie credits her choice of Roger with enabling her to rise to such a senior position. 'I know for a fact I couldn't have done it without him. It's hard enough to become senior as a research scientist whether you are a man *or* a woman, but his support has been invaluable.'

She continues: 'When I got my position of professor his immediate reaction was, "We did it!" We don't have any issues with the money because my success is a joint effort.' Interestingly, Roger was raised by a mother who worked outside the home, which in the 1960s may have helped enable him to see fluidity in traditional gender roles. She says: 'Roger's never been a competitive person. It could have been problematic if he felt threatened by my success.'

There was a period when the children were school age that Roger went back to work full-time in an office. 'It just didn't suit us, though; it was very tough. Sometimes I think I am a female chauvinist! Essentially I have benefited from having a *wife* all these years,' she laughs.

Maggie continues: 'It suits us both, because he never hugely enjoyed paid work and it means he can always make the children a priority. Ironically, at home we fall into fairly normal gender roles with him managing the money and doing most of the driving.' She smiles: 'We certainly never set out to be unconventional!'

When I comment to Maggie that their choices seemed smooth for both of them she retorts with a laugh: 'That's because you are meeting me now! Twenty years ago I would have probably said how difficult it all felt. There's always a sense of insecurity. Until I had a permanent academic post and tenure, I was always so uncertain of my standing.'

She continues: 'The gender issue is always there. You never get over the feeling you're not doing the job you *should* be doing, whether you are at home or at work. You never felt you were doing enough for the post-docs you were responsible for, or for your family.' Maggie is clear, however, that any stress she felt was never due to resentment from Roger; rather it was her own self-imposed sense of responsibility.

Maggie explains: 'One of the advantages of being a research scientist is that you can be flexible – and attend events like sports days. The big things I can be there for. Our choices have allowed us to live the lives we have wanted and do the best for our children.

'Several years ago, I was in Japan working with a young female Japanese research scientist. She was certainly in the minority. While I was there we talked candidly about balancing career and family. On the last day, she gave me a card that read, "I hope someday I marry a man as wonderful as your husband." I gave it to Roger when I got back. We have kept in touch and she indeed got married and had children and was adamant she would continue to work.'

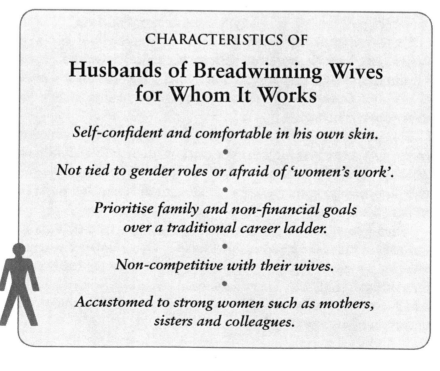

CHARACTERISTICS OF

Husbands of Breadwinning Wives for Whom It Works

Self-confident and comfortable in his own skin.

Not tied to gender roles or afraid of 'women's work'.

Prioritise family and non-financial goals over a traditional career ladder.

Non-competitive with their wives.

Accustomed to strong women such as mothers, sisters and colleagues.

6

THROUGH A DIFFERENT LENS: HOW FRIENDS AND FAMILY SEE FEMALE BREADWINNING

*'Of all the labour-saving devices ever invented for women,
none has ever been so popular as the devoted male.'*

LADIES HOME JOURNAL
1948

As I talked with female breadwinners, an interesting theme emerged. Men and women who had others who were supportive of the way they led their lives were much more comfortable in their non-traditional roles. For many men, the views of other people colour how they see their own situation. Men attach far greater importance to social comparisons, particularly with regard to their roles as providers and protectors of their families. This is in sharp contrast to women, who are more likely to derive self-esteem from the reflected appraisals of others.[94]

In short, men gain esteem by comparing themselves to other men, whereas women's source of esteem is from feedback.

Indeed, it is hard to ignore the judgements of others when they look at our lives. One of the first times I noticed this was when my husband and I were treating another couple to a meal. When I reached for the bill, they responded by looking at Geoff

---

[94] Schwalbe, ML & Staples, CL (1991) 'Gender differences in sources of self-esteem', *Social Psychology Quarterly*, 54, 158–168

with a smile and saying, 'Well, aren't you a lucky boy then!' The suggestion was that I was 'treating' Geoff. No doubt, if he had been paying, this couple would simply have seen him as 'providing' for me like a good husband.

Indeed when I mentioned this observation to several bread-winning women they said would let their husband pay, even if they would then have to top up his account to cover the expenditure. We can only change people's expectations if we stop colluding with this false image of manhood that ignores the reality for the sake of others' comfort. Clearly those around us send us implicit and sometimes explicit feedback about how they feel about their situation.

THROUGH THE EYES OF OTHERS

Female breadwinners were very aware of other's appraisals of their relatively unique situation. Questions of fairness and control were common from well-intentioned friends and family members. Several women mentioned that their own girlfriends had questioned their relationship. Quite understandably, when this happened they tended to feel defensive of their partners.

Daphne, now a partner in an accountancy firm, brings home over 90 per cent of their income. She says: 'I was telling a friend that you were going to interview me about being the main breadwinner and she remarked, "Daphne, you're the *only* breadwinner!"'

Daphne has grown accustomed to the idea she will always be the main earner in her relationship, but used to lament what she sees as Adrian's lack of initiative. She had a wake-up call when a friend asked her: 'Daphne, don't you realise you may eventually have to accept he's never going to be the career go-getter that you are?'

She smiles: 'At the time I didn't realise how wise she was. Now, I think that if you see a pattern early on in the relationship, you need to accept that that's the way it's likely to be long-term. If you are the sort of person who will resent the long hours you are working while your partner is not, then get out early. Your only other option is to focus on why, as the main breadwinner, your life is so much better with that person *not* working.' Daphne has accepted a situation which is unlikely to change.

Other people seemed to think the arrangement of female breadwinning as 'odd' and not one to emulate. Barbara is a private banker whose husband runs a loss-making adventure holiday business he loves. She explains: 'Friends have said I was too accommodating in the beginning taking charge, helping him along – and maybe they have a valid argument. I have given him an extremely comfortable life and perhaps he got *too* comfortable.'

The family live in the countryside, and Heinrich is away five months of the year hosting adventure tours in Africa. When asked about her social life during those months, Barbara wryly laughs: 'I live in a part of the country where no one wants a single woman at their dinner party on a Saturday night. I'm one of the only working mothers in the area. Women simply don't work in that neck of the woods.'

She elaborates: 'I hosted a charity coffee morning in our village a few weeks ago. One of the women in my town said to me, "Oh, Barbara, it's so interesting what you do! But I just want my daughter to do enough at school so she can marry well." A couple of other mothers chimed in saying the same thing. It's crazy because we are all paying huge fees to send our children, boys *and* girls, to these expensive schools! So I said, "Don't you think it would be great if your daughter followed a passion and worked at a job she loved?" They all said, "No, it's more important that she marries well, so her future is *secure*."'

Relating this story, Barbara was clearly dumbfounded by this response. The other mothers were plainly oblivious to the prevalence of modern divorce and the issues inherent in one partner being completely reliant on the other – a problem clearly illustrated by Barbara's own situation.

Heinrich's parents live in Austria and are estranged from each other, so they do not offer the family any support. Regarding her own family, Barbara admits: 'They're pretty horrified by our situation. My father feels very bad that he didn't sit Heinrich down before we married and ask if he could provide for me. Dad feels a lot of guilt about that.' Given that the couple had never anticipated Barbara being the sole provider in the long term, it is doubtful whether such a conversation would have made a huge impact in any case. To Heinrich, and indeed to most entrepreneurs, his business failing would not have seemed like a real possibility.

Barbara continues: 'I'm always careful to say that he is a very good father. My family and friends are civil to him on the rare occasions they see him. When I was in hospital recently, I was told to stop work for six months. With my responsibilities, I just couldn't do that. I think everyone hoped Heinrich would have stepped up at that point. He didn't. I think we all expected that, ten years on, if his business was not profitable, he would have found a job or done something part-time to contribute in some way.'

PROUD IN-LAWS

In some cases, the parents of female breadwinners focused much more on the success or happiness of their *sons-in-law*. Vashti and Terence are one such couple. Vashti is an airline security specialist. She is married to Terence, a consultant who travels to Germany every week for his job. Vashti's parents were immigrants from a small village in India. They came to the UK in the 1970s to work and taught themselves English. Her mother eventually got a PhD, and worked in cancer research. Vashti describes her family as blissfully unaware of their daughter's role as the main earner in the couple.

She says with a wry smile: 'They assume Terence does a lot better than me in earnings and in career status. When I tell them about my job they don't seem to relate to it. Terence has a loftier sounding title than I do, which probably contributes. I think they'd find it a little odd if we told them that I earned more than Terence. It doesn't fit their image of us. They are incredibly proud of him and think I married well.'

She quickly defends them saying: 'Don't get me wrong, they are proud of me, but they focus on *him*.' This was fascinating as I had to point out from our earlier conversation that her mother had a PhD and was *herself* the primary breadwinner for many years after her father retired. To this observation, Vashti's eyes widen and she answers: 'I never thought about it that way!'

Vashti remembers: 'A few years ago, when the airports were starting to have terrible queues after 9/11 and there was a lot of confusion about check-in times and what you could bring on board and what you couldn't, my parents came for lunch. While we were eating, they quizzed Terence as to what was going on with airports, probably because he flies a lot. But he's a retail consultant; he knows nothing about it!'

She continues: 'I didn't say anything about it at the time, but I remember thinking, "this is *my* job!" It's not like I keep what I do for a living a secret!' Vashti thinks her family's focus on Terence's success is generational as 'the older generation don't think about women earning this way.' While this may be true, it's striking how persistent these ideas remain *in spite* of the pattern of female breadwinning that worked for her own parents.

Maggie, a professor, is married to Roger, a stay-at-home father. She grew up in a very conventional family with her mother at home. Her father was a factory worker and neither went to university. It took Maggie's father a long time to accept that Roger was happy with his role in the home.

She says: 'I know Dad was very proud of me. But he would still take me aside and ask, "Is Roger all right? Is he happy?" They adore Roger. They slowly got used to seeing him do what they probably saw as *my* job. There was always a sense of "isn't Roger wonderful for staying at home?"'

UNIMPRESSED PARENTS

Like in-laws everywhere, other parents were less impressed by the men their daughters had chosen. They felt disappointment for their daughters and that they could have 'married better'. The assumption being that marrying 'better' meant marrying a high earner.

Maria is a Spanish banker who has lived and worked in the UK for 20 years. She lives with Elliott, an English composer, and their four children. They met when they were both students. She was studying in London for a summer and he was at Cambridge. His Oxbridge background seemed so glamorous she was charmed immediately.

Though they are the same age, Elliott acted as Maria's guide from the beginning, helping her understand the UK. He coached her in interview etiquette and how to make small talk. He essentially served as a cultural mentor who eased her into British life in her early twenties.

Maria was a serious student and not looking for a relationship when she arrived for her summer course. She jokes that within three days of meeting Elliott, she knew he was 'the one'. She remembers: 'I was always focused on what I was *supposed to do* to get good marks and a strong career. He did what he *wanted to do*. That was *so* fascinating to me.'

Elliott loved the arts and music and did amateur dramatics as well. He opened up a new world to Maria, who was studying economics and business management. After that first summer, she returned to Spain to tell her family she was moving back to the UK for good. Understandably, this was a huge shock to her mother and a departure from the cultural expectation of living with her family until she married. She laughs: 'I don't think my mother ever got over the surprise. She probably still hopes I will return and marry a proper Spaniard!'

Her father does not care that Elliott earns substantially less, but her mother has never taken to him, saying repeatedly that Maria deserves better. The 'better' is assumed to be someone who will financially provide for Maria and their children despite the fact that Maria earns a healthy six-figure salary herself.

She elaborates: 'When the children came along we had been a couple for twelve years. Only then did she start to come to terms with the fact that Elliott wasn't going anywhere.'

WITH FRIENDS LIKE THESE, WHO NEEDS ENEMIES?

The influence of others is strong, and many people feel free to comment on the benefits or drawbacks of a couple's situation as they see it. Female breadwinners said that friends often felt free to pass judgement on their situation. Over a quarter (26 per cent) of the breadwinning wives surveyed by *Redbook* magazine in 2010 said that friends or family had remarked that they thought their situation was odd.[95] Other women said their partners received comments about their situation that ranged from praise and jealousy to confusion with their choice and even condescension.

It is amazing how powerful others' perceptions are in shaping how we feel about our lives. The men who struggled most were those subject to criticism from others outside the relationship. As one woman explains: 'I can tell when he's been spending time with certain "friends". If we argue, he will retort: "Don't emasculate me!" as if I am being too controlling. I know our set-up has soured a few of his past friendships.'

On the other hand, I heard of male friends remarking how lucky a man is to have found a woman who out-earns him, enabling him to follow a career he is passionate about or to spend more time with his children. Other male friends expressed surprise that any man would be happy with such an 'emasculating' relationship. Needless to say, men who received favourable comments adapted to the status of being the lower earner or stay-at-home partner much better than men whose friends and family questioned their masculinity.

MINE'S BIGGER THAN YOURS: COMPARISONS WITH OTHER MEN

Sometimes it is the comparison with other male friends that can make or break a man's perception of his role.

Such was the case for Grace and Dan. Grace runs her own public relations consultancy outside Glasgow and is married to Dan. When they met in their twenties, she was enjoying a fast track career in PR. Dan worked in the automotive industry for many years, never hugely enjoying his work but always aware of the path that was expected of him.

---

[95] Goad, K 'Big Earning Wives, and the Men Who Love Them', MSN Lifestyle, September 13, 2010

Grace says: 'His closest university friends have done very well in business, but I could tell his heart was never in it. He was a square peg in a round hole.' This comparison led to an uncomfortable period of questioning for Dan. As I talk with Grace, I realise their frequent and honest communication is one of the keys to success in their relationship.

She explains: 'I think men have a tough time. They are conditioned to be the main person who brings home the money. They see other men taking that mantle on and compare themselves. At the end of the day, we are all individuals and that responsibility doesn't suit everyone.'

Grace elaborates: 'Women may struggle with the decision to work or be at home, but men also struggle with their sense of identity. Now that more women are becoming the main breadwinners, it enables men to think about what they want out of life rather than blindly assuming they have to work at a dull job for the rest of their days. They have a new freedom to say, "I'm not sure I fit that alpha male stereotype. It's okay not to want to be the CEO."'

She says: 'He went through a period of being really despondent about his options. He would look around at all the guys ahead of him in corporate life and say, "You know, Grace, none of them seem to smile. They don't laugh enough and I just don't aspire to that." He's such a fabulous guy, really funny and personable. I hated what this expectation to be the "big man" was doing to him.

'He's extremely loyal to us, but I realised something had to change the day after our first daughter was born. He said with this sense of resignation, "Okay, I'm in this job for life, I just have to think about how I am going to make the most of it."'

In the years after their first daughter arrived, it became increasingly obvious Dan was in the wrong career. Grace says: 'Once he recognised I was willing to take on the responsibility and he didn't have to be a wage slave, he became a lot more confident about his status in the marriage. He was also less resentful of me and the success of his friends.' Interestingly, for many men the issue of self-esteem could be a challenge if a man had low regard for his own work.

Grace, on the other hand, was keen to return to work after having her second child. While on her second maternity leave, she remembers: 'I really struggled with not bringing money into the household and losing my status as income generator. I actually love to work.' Grace and Dan's turning point came the day before she went into labour with their second child. Timing is everything, and Dan chose that moment to announce he wanted to start his own bespoke cabinetry business. Grace laughs as she remembers shouting, '*Now* is the time to tell me this?'

They compromised and decided he would stay in his corporate role for one more year while she was on maternity leave. At the same time, he would do further woodwork training before she would take up the reins with full-time work.

She says: 'People think I'm so great for taking this on. Actually, once he realised what he wanted to do, he was so much happier and a lot easier to be around.' Grace now brings in two-thirds of their income, and she explains: 'He may earn hardly anything compared to his old job, but he's the envy of all his friends who commute to Edinburgh and Glasgow while he drives around in a beat-up old van, taking on the jobs that interest him.'

> *In-laws can be very judgemental, confusing*
> *'marrying well' with 'marrying rich'.*
>
> •
>
> *Supportive male friends were vital to men*
> *who are not the main earners.*
>
> •
>
> *Men frequently compare their successes to*
> *other men they know.*

One of the main benefits of Dan's change into cabinet making was the way it allowed him to stop comparing himself with his peers. She reflects: 'I think the best thing we have done is to recognise that the CEO model doesn't fit everyone. Dan was allowed to define success on his own terms.'

It is this constant discussion around values and remaining very clear about what success is *for them* that keeps this couple so grounded.

MOTHER KNOWS BEST: MEN WITH BREADWINNING MOTHERS

The roles we see our parents take as we grow up undoubtedly has a big impact on how we develop our own roles later in life. Just think how many of your parenting skills and values were picked up from your own parents. It could be suggested that a man whose mother worked might be more comfortable married to a female breadwinner, but I didn't always find this to be the case. Some women were encouraged to work by their husbands for a variety of reasons, often as a direct reaction to how they were raised.

Allison, a management consultant, says: 'Ironically, George's mother stayed at home. He always wanted a smart and independent wife who would work and use her brain. He knows he was lucky to have her at home, but thinks she could have made a much larger contribution to the world. He wanted a wife who would use her full potential. In some ways he probably got more than he bargained for!'

At the other extreme, Heinrich, Barbara's husband, came from the same model he now inhabits – his mother worked because his father would not. His father had been due to inherit land and a peerage, confiscated during World War II. Losing the family wealth was a huge psychological blow to him, and he never worked. Instead, Heinrich's mother took up the breadwinning mantle and worked for the Foreign Service.

Barbara thinks Heinrich's aristocratic background may play a part in how he views work. She says: 'I think he's felt victimised. His father should have inherited this great big estate and then Heinrich in turn would have inherited it. There is a sense of helplessness from them both, a feeling of "poor me", but no one from the family has even tried to recover the assets. I hope to God our son doesn't inherit his attitude.'

WHAT ABOUT HIS PARENTS?

While the decision for the man's career to take the back seat may be straightforward for some couples, it is sometimes not readily accepted by *his* family, whose reaction could only be described as antagonistic. Some families are concerned over the amount of control they feel the wife may have over her husband because of his dependent financial status. Others are just disappointed because being the secondary breadwinner or at-home father is simply not the life they wished for their son.

To this end, for many years, Jackie's mother-in-law made snide comments about her son 'wasting' his education since he now watched their children full-time. For years the couple, who were themselves very happy with the arrangement, largely ignored her disapproval. Eventually, however, her complaints became too much for Jackie.

She describes: 'One Saturday night, I was driving her to a party – taking time out of my evening to take her a 60-mile round trip, and as usual she started complaining. So I said, "I think you should know I earn four times what Donald earned at the top of his career. Without my earnings we couldn't take you on all the family holidays we do. And what about the value of *my* education? Should that be 'wasted'?" I haven't heard a peep from her since.'

Jackie says: 'My own mother adores Donald. Even so, if anything goes wrong with the kids, she will insinuate that if *I* were at home, perhaps we wouldn't have had problems.'

Melanie's in-laws were similarly unhappy about her being the breadwinner even from the start of their relationship. When they were engaged, Connor enrolled on a postgraduate degree while living with his fiancée. His parents were worried he would be beholden to Melanie and she would have an 'unnatural' amount of control. This of course begs the questions, what is a 'natural' amount of control and would they have objected if *he* had had the perceived control?

Melanie says: 'He came from a strong Catholic background, and his family was disappointed on several levels: he was living in sin, living off me, and not attending Mass! We just didn't look at it that way. Even from the beginning we approached it as a partnership. I think the key was that we had started out as best friends, which is why it's been a success all the way through. We trust each other. Everything is shared.'

After completing his graduate degree, Connor worked full-time for many years, even when the children were young. However, he eventually gave up paid work to become at-home father to their children. Much of his initial self-doubt about the role came from his perceptions of how others, particularly his mother, viewed him.

Regarding his stay-at-home role, Melanie says: 'Connor's mother would say, "This is an interesting experiment, but when are you going to get on with finding a *real* job?" I have had to repeatedly say to her that while I'm a woman, I don't do secretarial work and I earn well enough for him to stay home. To her, the only real jobs are doctor, lawyer and accountant. In her eyes, her children are failures because only one of them is an accountant.' Melanie's mother-in-law often remarks that Melanie should be the one at home, ignoring the reality that Melanie earns more than Connor ever did.

It is not surprising that couples sometimes face criticism about the choices they make, particularly when the couples themselves have often experienced tension *within* the relationship over their non-traditional roles. While I have highlighted some of the backlash that can come from others regarding the female breadwinner model, these instances were in the minority.

More than half of the women I spoke with had families and in-laws who were supportive about the choices the couple had made, recognising it made sense for all involved. This might be some of the best evidence that, as a society, women are making some of their *fastest* progress in changing attitudes within the family.

In just a few decades, people have begun to accept that women can be the main breadwinner and that their husbands need not be emasculated bundles of self-doubt.

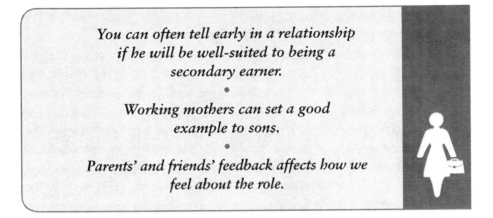

You can often tell early in a relationship if he will be well-suited to being a secondary earner.

•

Working mothers can set a good example to sons.

•

Parents' and friends' feedback affects how we feel about the role.

UNMET EXPECTATIONS

Allison, a management consultant and mother of a toddler son, says: 'I never thought of George as a great breadwinner when we were dating, but I knew instinctively that when he found his niche he would do very well. I never thought, *show me the money!*' She laughs: 'George is a late bloomer. It might take some time, but he has drive. Plus he's very optimistic and a bit of a risk-taker, which I'm not. It's probably one of the things that drew me to him.'

Allison remembers: 'When we met, I was still at university so George was the main earner. Soon after we married, we were both made redundant. I managed to find contracting work, but George didn't. For the first four years he worked on and off fairly regularly, but in the last few years it's been less consistent. He sometimes makes a financial contribution, but we can't count on it.' George provides childcare for their son two days a week and works on the business the other three. Allison explains: 'When the switch in our roles happened, we thought it was just temporary –

but five years on, we're still doing it!'

When asked whether she thought it would continue, she deeply sighs and says: 'I hope not, or he will go insane! He is completely bored at the moment. George's not the kind of person who can be unemployed. He wavers between wanting to find full-time employment and growing a new business. I know he will get work. But to be honest, until he finds his niche, I will probably be the breadwinner for the foreseeable future.'

Allison sighs: 'Being the main breadwinner didn't always bother me. Now that we have Alexander, I expected to be the main carer. I planned on still working part-time and I was looking forward to that.' Ironically, her husband George looks after Alexander but would prefer to be working and Allison would prefer to be looking after Alexander. 'I realise how lucky I was to have my mother at home with me. I wanted the same for our children, and I assumed it would be me at home. I miss him during the day, but it's just me missing him, he's certainly not suffering. He gets George who obviously loves him a lot. I always knew I wanted the best childcare for our child, but now I realise he *is* getting the best childcare he can. I just always thought it would be me providing it.'

It is worth mentioning that Allison is the only woman I spoke to out of dozens who would prefer to be the main carer for her child – but even she still wanted to work outside the home.

LETTING GO OF THE CINDERELLA COMPLEX

Do female breadwinners, even those who are primarily happy with their role, ever wish they could be rescued from the responsibility? Actually, very few do.

The fantasy of how we would spend our time if we didn't have to earn occurs to all working people, in much the same way that people love to speculate what they would do after a lottery win. I don't think such fantasies speak to a lack of a feminist work ethic, but they do show a natural curiosity about lives not lived. I suspect a fair number of men would think having women they could financially rely on would be equally attractive. Again, what is key is the idea of *choice*. The women most likely to wish they could be rescued from financial responsibility are those who don't realistically have that option.

Daphne, a partner in an accountancy practice, smiles when she recalls: 'I recently saw a childhood friend for the first time in 20 years. In the time we'd been apart she had met a wealthy man at a dinner party, married him and become a Lady! She actually lives in a castle and has five children.' She laughs as she continues: 'Now, I love my job, but why don't I get invited to those types of dinner parties? Sometimes I wonder what it would be like not to have to go to work, and to have someone to look after me for the rest of my life.'

As rare as it is to become the rescued 'Cinderella', the fantasy belies the high divorce rate in Western countries. *Kept women* who experience divorce are extremely vulnerable. . . just the same as *kept men*. Daphne elaborates: 'I'm the type of woman who likes working. As much as I may try and pin the fact that I *have* to work on Adrian on my down days, I know I would do it anyway.'

In fact, other female breadwinners knew that their situation would continue for a variety of reasons. The main reason was the new reliance they had on their husbands to run the household and watch the children in an era of rising childcare costs. In short, these men would not earn well enough to offset the day-to-day costs of working.

For example, Linda, who works as a consultant, cannot imagine Brian returning to work. They live in a remote village which makes finding any kind of local work virtually impossible. She says: 'He's not exactly champing at the bit to return to the world of work, but even if he was to take on any work locally, the pay would not be good enough for him to make up the childcare costs we would have to bear.'

Likewise, Elise, an architect, knows she will always be the main breadwinner for two reasons. She explains: 'Lionel was never passionate about his career in banking to begin with so he'd never go back to that. Plus, now he's been out of the market so long, he'd have to re-train in another area.' Lionel has not shown any interest in retraining. Therefore, his day-to-day care of their children means that the most important financial contribution he can make is within the home.

My conclusion is that we may as well throw away the Cinderella Complex. The benefit of having a stay-at-home partner is the support they offer *at home*. He is unlikely ever to become a driven, alpha-male breadwinner, which is probably a big part of what you loved about him from the start. The happiest women I met were those who accepted that they had the scope for achieving higher earnings and that it was their choice to manifest that potential by being the main breadwinner.

ACCEPTING THE ROLE OF FEMALE BREADWINNER

Daphne and Adrian, who are unmarried, have been together fifteen years. She recalls: 'I was working flat-out all week as a trainee accountant in London and going a million miles a minute. I liked how laid-back Adrian was about everything. It was a real change for me.' She jokes: 'I can't say I was ever misled. I knew from day one that he only ever worked to live, and would do as little as he could to get by.'

She explains: 'He's never been career-minded and for the first ten years I found that intensely frustrating, like he needed a kick up the backside! He's an intelligent guy but doesn't have any formal qualifications. At the beginning, I would always push him to better himself. Technically he's self-employed. He works odd days for a removal company, but the truth is he doesn't do much of that either. This week, for example, he's moving a family into a new house, but that's from a contact *I* knew!'

The couple have no children, but Adrian contributes by running the household. Daphne says: 'I do the cooking, but he manages the house and garden. He also plays a huge amount of sport. I used to think maybe sport was his professional calling, but whenever he does relief coaching for a youth team he comes home complaining about how stressful it is.'

While Daphne used to encourage Adrian to be more ambitious,

she has stopped in the last few years for several reasons. Her work hours are long and her schedule erratic. When a project comes to an end, she likes to travel with Adrian but often at very short notice. She explains: 'He often points out that not having a nine-to-five job suits *me* because it means we can take off on last-minute breaks. In fact, there was a short spell when he had a more regular job. Once we couldn't take a pre-paid holiday to Thailand because of the inflexibility of his holiday entitlement. That was very annoying, particularly since he didn't love the job.'

In the weeks prior to our interview, Adrian had had an unusually busy spell of house removals. This made Daphne reflective and she says: 'It's given me pause for thought for couples who both work long hours every day. It's tough when both partners come home tired and grouchy. If they have children, it must be all the more stressful. We have a much higher quality of life with him not working. The domestic things are done, and we can use our weekends for fun. Plus Adrian wouldn't earn very much anyway, even if he did have a regular job.'

His lack of formal qualifications means that any regular income he could earn from a stable job would not be worth the hassle of his unavailability.

There is a second, and perhaps more significant reason why Daphne no longer pushes Adrian to work full-time. After struggling with infertility for several years, Daphne was diagnosed with uterine cancer. She remembers: 'The infertility caused the biggest rows in our relationship. It wasn't that he didn't want children, but he didn't want to be the main caregiver. But it was obvious I couldn't do it either! His heart wasn't in it. I was the one pushing the agenda.'

She sighs: 'It's extremely stressful and I know a good number of other couples who broke up because of the pressure.' His reluctance raised questions about responsibilities in a relationship, an issue encountered by several other couples. How do you reconcile giving up both the breadwinning role and also eschewing the parenting role – two responsibilities most adults take on as a matter of course?

For most couples, doing the childcare justified the man taking on the at-home role. In my interviews, Adrian and Daphne were the only couple where he primarily stayed at home but there were no children to care for.

In fact, her devastating cancer created a real turning point for the relationship. Adrian became her pillar of support. She explains: 'I was going to the hospital every day for nearly a year. He never complained once. He was always at my side. I was so sick and didn't know what I wanted to eat or what I wanted to do each day. He was just fantastic. He was a real rock, and didn't make any fuss about it. In fact, he is now doing the same for his mother who is unfortunately very ill. He just gets on it with it.'

Her cancer, which came hard on the heels of her fertility treatment, may in fact have salvaged the relationship. Adrian stepped up, not as a parent, as she would have anticipated just a few months before, but as a *partner*. The relationship has subsequently mellowed. Daphne says: 'I have become calmer over time, and we have just accepted that we won't have children. We have become more accepting and less critical of each other as individuals. We're in a good place.'

Being the Female Breadwinner May Work For You If You Are:

Happy to continue your career until retirement.

•

Raised as a girl to be independent.

•

Accustomed to bucking convention by working in a male-dominated field or are self-employed.

•

Confident in your career direction.

•

Realise everyone's got an opinion but you don't have to accept it.

•

Are drawn to men for their personality rather than their earning potential.

7

STUMBLING BLOCKS

'The Golden Rule works for men as written, but for women it should go the other way around. We need to do unto ourselves as we do for others.'

GLORIA STEINEM

As in any other relationship, couples which had a female breadwinner had their share of ups and downs. There are myriad ways people relate to each other, and I was able to witness both the ways people make these arrangements work for them, and the problems they encounter along the way.

In the next two chapters, we will look at some of the stumbling blocks women faced when negotiating with their lesser earning partners. Certainly there could be real issues, as one might expect around the power dynamics and taking on non-traditional roles. However, a good number of the problems faced by women breadwinners are those faced by most working women – regardless of how much they earn. This was refreshing as it suggested that having a high earning wife did not lead to problems in itself.

In chapter nine, we will look at the ways forward and how you can make these relationships work well for you and your family.

DRAGGING HIS HEELS:
RELUCTANCE AT HOUSEWORK

Perhaps it was not surprising that housework was such a sticking point for many couples; after all, this is an issue on which most couples, no matter who is the main earner, cannot always agree. Female breadwinners employ a variety of strategies to get the household help they need. Many said they had to explicitly and repeatedly convince their partners that doing their share of housework and childcare was as valuable as a paycheque.

Tensions arose when men didn't believe they were valued, or indeed when female breadwinners did not think they were getting enough help domestically from their partner.[96]

Carly and Luke typified this struggle. Carly is a senior research scientist in the field of degenerative diseases. She and Luke have been married for twelve years and have two young children. He works full-time in hospital administration. They met when she was a PhD student. Soon after she graduated he decided to do his PhD while she worked. Luke continued on this path for two years before realising academia wasn't a good fit, and moved back into the work world.

In their first few years together, their earnings were roughly equivalent, but in the last six years Carly has brought home 60 per cent of the family income. Luke has spent that time alternating between self-employment and two unfulfilling positions he resigned from, which in itself caused problems.

Carly says: 'I knew he wasn't completely happy in those roles, but he just resigned without talking to me beforehand. Knowing I'm there to pay the mortgage makes it easier for him to be impulsive.' Carly's secure salary means she feels she can't take the kind of career risks Luke feels he can. She laments: 'He compares every other job to his first job, and that's a big problem. I have brought it up subtly with him, but I don't feel I can be completely honest.'

Obviously, having a partner whose employment is stable and

---

[96] Meisenbach, R (2010) 'The female breadwinner: Phenomenological experience and gendered identity in work/family spaces', *Sex Roles*, 62, 2–19

well-paying means the other partner can take more career risks. It only leads to resentment if the main provider feels they themselves cannot take advantage of the opportunities they would enjoy.

The tension between the couple was exacerbated by Luke's reluctance to increase his domestic workload, particularly during his spells of unemployment. Carly sighs: 'I would get the children up, feed them, take them to school and pick them up. When we'd get home no laundry had been done or food prepared and he would just say, "I was busy. I read an interesting book." I know he had to be reflective for a while, but it got to be very frustrating because he loved to remind me he was "wearing the knickers in the house" since I was the one earning.'

Having her salary plus the domestic workload she takes on used against her as evidence of 'emasculation' was understandably difficult for Carly and caused resentment.

Many couples go into their relationship able to practise equality in the household tasks early on. Like other new parents, Carly and Luke found that, after the arrival of their children, they fell into more set gender patterns. She remembers: 'I think he found it difficult to do the cleaning and cooking because it was "women's work".'

As other research indicates, Carly credits Luke with contributing more to the housework when he is *working full-time as well*. I think that for men going through a period of underemployment or unemployment, doing the washing and other 'women's work' is adding insult to injury during a time when they are already questioning their sense of identity and contribution.

Those eighteen months while Luke was out of work were particularly difficult as he suffered from depression and became cynical. Carly says: 'I don't think it was ever about me earning more, rather it was about him contributing *less*. He lost a lot of the confidence I'd always loved about him. He was short-tempered and he would throw my long hours back at me. I gritted my teeth so I wouldn't yell back, "Well, one of us has to bring in the money."'

Carly would ideally like to spend more time with the children, but unless there is a major shift for Luke, she knows she will be the main breadwinner for the long term. She sighs: 'I can't seem to win either way. I spend time at home and think I should be doing more at work but when I give the hours to my job, I'm resentful I can't be with the kids.'

WHO'S THE BIGGEST BABY IN THE HOUSE?

There was a tendency for some men to take up at-home childcare *after* their children were school age. For some, this was because managing children's diaries with two full-time workers finally became too difficult, or wives only reached a salary where they could support a whole family once their children were older.

However, I also think that men were more honest about not wanting to take on the day-to-day care of babies – recognising the sheer difficulty of the responsibility.

Many women were happy to mix day-to-day care from an at-home father with multiple days in nursery, recognising that both the child and father would need a break. I couldn't help but wonder if parents would be so generous about nursery care when women are stay-at-home mothers. There was a sense that men needed a break from small babies and it was in the family's best interest to facilitate that freedom.

I wondered whether this was because women themselves knew how difficult they would find unbroken childcare on a daily basis, or if regular spells in nursery was one way to get men to commit or feel better about taking on the at-home role.

Maureen, who runs a successful PR agency, points out that when their daughter Sarah was a baby, most of the responsibilities were hers alone. She says: 'I was the one who wanted Sarah because Bill had already had two children from a previous marriage. Though I was working full-time and Bill wasn't, it was pretty clear she was my responsibility. Luckily, as she got older, and more interesting to be around, she charmed him and now he enjoys spending time with her.'

Maureen managed through Sarah's early years with plenty of support from her mother, who visited when Maureen had to be away for several days at a time. She says: 'The beauty of having your own business is that I could work from home when Sarah was sick. It's funny because people often think childcare is easier when they are in school. When they are babies at least crèche is available most days of the year, so you don't have to worry about school holidays, half-days and half-terms. It's actually become much more difficult as she has become older, so it's a good thing that Bill takes more interest in her now!'

Bill, who is a freelance writer, now does 70 per cent of the school runs. Maureen says: 'He sometimes complains he can't seek full-time work somewhere because he has to be so flexible for her schedule.' She pauses heavily before continuing: 'But I actually think it suits him better than he lets on. He can go to the gym, see a friend for lunch and do a little bit of writing before she comes home. At the moment he's fed up with work. Sometimes he complains he can't retrain to do something else because of Sarah. I know we could manage it if he were truly interested in another career, but I don't think he actually is.'

Maureen recognises the conundrum this presents, however, as she says: 'We couldn't both work the hours I do; Sarah would get neglected. So, while I might resent it at times, I know it serves us all.'

A FUTURE RISE IN MALE DEPRESSION?

As I talk with many of the women, I am aware how much personal status is linked to one's job. This can be a particular issue for couples where he earns significantly less or is primarily in an at-home role, *and feels badly* about that differentiation. Men may have traditionally seen their contributions to household management as very secondary to their primary role as breadwinner.

Some researchers warn of an impending surge in the number of men suffering from depression. They credit two main causes: a de-stigmatization around men expressing their feelings and the rise of the female breadwinner who, by default it would seem, emasculates men and their traditional identity.[97]

---

[97] Dunlop, B & Mletzko, T (2011) 'Will current socioeconomic trends produce a depressing future for men?', editorial in *British Journal of Psychiatry*, 198, 16–168

The anecdotal research these stories are drawn from comes from doctors consulting for pharmaceutical companies and shows *no actual evidence* of any increase in depression levels. Nevertheless, women stealing men's role as breadwinner certainly incites scaremongering headlines such as 'Male Depression Will Rise', as if female breadwinning can only lead to a bleak future.[98] Certainly, the incidence of male depression may rise in years to come – but if so, it will arise from a whole range of reasons.

However, the prevalence of *female* depression due to a lack of a meaningful role outside of motherhood was historically a non-issue. Betty Friedan was the first to discuss the vast numbers of well-educated but unfulfilled women in the 1950s who suffered from 'the problem with no name'. In her seminal text *The Feminine Mystique* she recognised that a lack of purposeful work and sense of independent identity contributed to depression in women[99] – the same issue some speculate with *no evidence* will 'plague' men in years to come.

> *Men taking on a lesser-earning role, against their will, may be slow to pick up domestic chores.*
>
> •
>
> *Fathers are often more willing to take on an at-home role after children are in school.*
>
> •
>
> *Rates of depression may rise among modern men - but is not a foregone conclusion.*

---

[98] thismorning.itv.com/thismorning/health/male-depression-will-rise
[99] Friedan, B (1963) *The Feminine Mystique*, New York, Dell Publishing

WHO AM I? FORGING A NEW IDENTITY

Almost as if to offset a concern over identity and depression, many women were quick to point out that their husbands are *not* stay-at-home fathers. Instead, they are setting up a consultancy, starting up a business, playing the money markets, even though, to all intents and purposes, they take on the primary care-giving role to children.

Naming another activity with which men engage also reinforces the idea that the decision to be the partner at home may be temporary and that they primarily do something *else*: something of higher status to the outside world. It is not an ongoing identity. It is less threatening to denote himself first as something in addition to stay-at-home father, rather than publicly taking on such an undervalued role in our society.

Men who were home all day were described as freelance website designers, IT consultants, fledgling entrepreneurs, day traders, amateur fix-it men. I am in no way denying that these other roles exist or denigrating the meaning they have for the men. What is interesting is how important it was for the men to have these titles in addition to their at-home role.

I would also argue that there is increasing pressure on women to be 'more' than stay-at-home mothers. The status of full-time parents has decreased for both men and women. Taking on alternative identities is not just about protecting their image to others, but also to themselves.

Alain de Botton talked about this need for identity through work in *The Pleasures and Sorrows of Work*: 'Our choice of occupation is held to define our identity to the extent that the most insistent question we ask of new acquaintances is not where they come from or who their parents were but what they do. The assumption being that the route to meaningful existence must invariably pass through the gate of remunerative employment.'[100]

Jackie and Donald are a prime example of how a multiplicity of roles works well for people who take on the at-home role.

---

[100] De Botton, Alain (2009) *The Pleasures and Sorrows of Work*, Penguin, p 96

Jackie, whose husband raised their children while also working part-time at home, says: 'I think it takes a very special man to do what Donald did.' What does she mean by 'special'? She sighs: 'Looking after children can be quite boring, and there's a huge loss of status! I didn't realise it myself until I had to retire early for health reasons. When people ask you "what do you do?" they always mean your paid work, and without a good answer, they are just not interested. I make a point now not to ask people that question any more.'

Donald worked part-time until he was made redundant through a company merger. Jackie said it never occurred to him to look for another job, since she earned well and he enjoyed cooking and managing the house. She says: 'The only thing that annoyed him was that he didn't get invited to coffee mornings by other mothers, not even by women he saw regularly through the children's playdates.'

Loss of status can be problematic for many men who newly find themselves in a secondary role. If they are unable to discover new and fulfilling roles, or don't value their at-home role, it can challenge both the way they identify themselves and the value they ascribe to what they are contributing.

Fortunately, Donald made the most of his sporting hobbies, playing football until he was 45 and taking on various roles within his local football club. Jackie says: 'I don't think he's ever thought, *I need a sense of masculine identity!*, But he certainly loves the time he spends at the club. He is very involved in its day-to-day running. He is a real man's man.'

It strikes me that, as a former player standing over six foot two, his involvement in the running of a football club may help insulate Donald from the identities of masculine crisis some men suffer when taking on a traditionally feminine role. Clearly a confident man, Donald found status in a variety of roles both at home and in his extracurricular activities.

FINDING THE WAY HOME:
MEN AND LOSS OF DIRECTION

For some couples, problems arose when the man could not find a sense of direction for his career. Certainly, discovering a sense of professional purpose is challenging for most people. However, some women felt that their being the primary breadwinner may have contributed to the length of time it took for the men to find their feet in the work world, or to the frequency with which they left it.

This perception could be validated by the career success they went on to have *after* she was no longer willing to foot the bill.

Susan met her first husband, Stefano, in Italy when she was studying there. After her studies, they returned to the US to find work for both of them. She remembers: 'Stefano was very open to the idea of living in the US, but we soon realised he couldn't easily find work if we didn't get married. It forced a decision we thought we would take sooner or later anyway.'

Things were moving quickly for the couple. At 24, and just a year after getting married, Susan was unexpectedly pregnant with their first child. Stefano had been a manual labourer in Italy but wanted to change professions after emigrating. He worked in various temporary jobs, but when Susan became pregnant, in the midst of establishing her own successful research business, Stefano offered to be the parent at home.

After their son, Giulio, was eighteen months old, he began to attend day care in order to free up Stefano's time for further education and training. She says: 'At that point, my company was doing well and money wasn't the main issue. I encouraged him to think of several different training programmes, but he just wouldn't commit to anything. After a year of him half-heartedly attending a range of classes, we decided it would be the ideal time to have the second child we wanted because he could take care of her.'

A year later their daughter Sarah was born. Susan worked from home while Stefano watched the children and attended courses. This arrangement worked well when the children were little.

As the children grew, however, Stefano still did not find a new professional direction. Susan says: 'By the time Giulio started school, I felt as if I couldn't keep having babies just to give him something to do! While it would have been fine if he wanted to commit to being a full-time stay-at-home dad, Stefano was clear he didn't formally want that responsibility either.'

Susan remembers that Stefano actually enjoyed the period when the children were little and he was the full-time carer, but he was never willing to commit to it fully. She says: 'He had plenty of confidence and never seemed embarrassed by telling people about the mix of things he did, but it went on too long. That's when I started to feel I had three children, not two.'

In hearing her story I realised that, whilst Stefano actually did much of the day-to-day childcare, he didn't want that label. Admitting to yourself and others that you are taking on the at-home role means accepting this is your new identity – which may be too uncomfortable for some.

The couple started marriage counselling which they attended for more than two years. Susan says: 'I didn't mind if he pumped gas for the rest of his life, as long as pumping gas was what he was passionate about! We weren't even 30 yet and I just wanted a partner who would develop and grow as a person. It was driving me crazy! I'd come home, make dinner with the kids around my ankles and he'd be just reading the paper even though he didn't have them all day while they were at school.'

After seven years together, the couple parted amicably. Susan even found him his first house-share after they separated. She remembers: 'It was priceless: the house-share was in our neighbourhood and the advert read, *Two divorced dads looking for third divorced dad!*'

The couple are still friendly. She explains: 'He spent last Christmas with us. He even still routinely sees my mother as they both live in Nevada. There is a part of me that will always love him. He's engaging and a really fun person. He wasn't a great partner, but he is a fantastic father. He didn't want the split, but he probably knew it was the best thing for us both. My mindset when we got married was that "this is it for good"; but how much can you know at 23?'

It's a bitter irony for Susan that only after the couple divorced did Stefano find a career he liked. In the fifteen years since their split, he has built a thriving osteopathy practice that all started from the first class he took after leaving their home. She reflects: 'He went on to work with many celebrities and has carved out a fantastic career for himself. Why couldn't he do that when we were together? If he had begun building up the business he has now, we probably would still be married today.'

She says: 'He's never been very ambitious and even now, even though he has a Rolodex full of famous clients, he works to get just enough money to live, rather than looking to build something larger.' This isn't simply an issue of his ambition not matching his wife's. Susan is clear that she only wanted him to be growing and learning *whilst* they were together.

Similarly to Josephine's or Barbara's story, Stefano was reluctant to act on any of his wife's advice. Susan says: 'I could make suggestions, but he would just go in the opposite direction. It got to a point where I could say, "What a beautiful sunny day," and he would find the one cloud in the sky.

'I often wonder if he felt he couldn't live up to me. Being Italian and quite proud, perhaps he needed to earn as much as me, but couldn't figure out how. He never liked school, so doing a professional qualification was never going to be the answer.'

The interview is emotional for Susan. She recognises that, had they stayed married, it is unlikely Stefano would have ever had the impetus to start his business. She says: 'I don't think I realised that ambition would have been a pre-requisite to a happy marriage. We had a great connection. I discovered it's vital that the man I'm with really *lives;* he engages with life. While Stefano never sat still when we were in Italy, he just became a different person who had no direction, and he didn't seem particularly concerned about it.'

In Susan's case there was deep remorse over the feeling of 'Why couldn't he step up when we were *together?*' – particularly in light of the successful life Stefano went on to lead. This lingering question was compounded by a shade of self-blame. She asks: 'Was his retreat because *I* am self-sufficient and ambitious?'

So, what if these women had been *less* than they are: less

ambitious, less well-paid, less optimistic about their own careers? That is clearly not the answer either. As Susan says in a deadpan voice: 'If I'd been less ambitious, he never would've been interested in me.' In fact, Susan says that Stefano's relationships *after* her have all been with women just as career-minded as she.

The irony is that what attracts us to someone is often what drives us apart later. Someone who is 'kind' becomes 'soft'; an 'ambitious' woman becomes a 'workaholic'; a 'focused' man becomes 'dogmatic'.

IN PRAISE OF VOLUNTEERING

Several of the men who didn't work for pay became very involved in the local community. The involvement of fathers in local school activities must be a boon to the education and charitable sectors, both of which are industries that have seen a significant drop in volunteers since more women have gone to work full-time.

Like some of the other fathers, Lionel began volunteering at his children's school as soon as they were old enough to attend.

Elise says: 'His time there evolved, but now he's there every day. He effectively does the job of a teaching assistant. He's also the chair of the Parent Teacher Association. The school loves him, and it's given him a chance to shine and a sense of satisfaction. He will drop the girls off, come home and do some tidying, before going back to spend the rest of the day there. I joke with him that nothing ever gets done around the house, and that they should put him on the payroll. But it's fine.'

In effect, Lionel has taken on an unpaid part-time job at the school. Elise and Lionel have even discussed whether he would consider teaching professionally. Elise smiles: 'He has come around to the idea that teaching might not be such a bad idea. It would certainly help me feel less angst about us being completely reliant on me. I've only ever felt that way since the economy has dipped. If the market improved, I probably wouldn't mind so much.'

The family works to a budget. She says: 'We joke that the kids get their pocket money and Lionel gets his pocket money. We don't do debt. We have a mortgage and that's it. I get cash ahead of time when I know he will need it, so he doesn't have to ask me. Otherwise, he just uses our joint account. He doesn't spend wildly, but we try to make sure he gets his nights out with other dads. Sunday mornings are sacrosanct for golf with his mates.'

Certainly, for many men, involvement in local sports clubs, school and community activities offered a place to use the skills they first honed in the workplace, plus a new and appreciative audience for their efforts.

WHEN ENOUGH IS ENOUGH

Susan's second husband, Thomas, whom she met two years later, was completely different from Stefano. He was driven, high-energy, career-focused. Additionally, she laughs: 'Stefano was skinny and short; Thomas was six feet tall and beefy. You felt safe when he hugged you!' She deeply respected his career progression and fondly says: 'He knew how to make the impossible happen and never took no for an answer.'

It is no doubt the fact that Thomas seemed to be a polar opposite to Stefano would have been wildly attractive to Susan. It was a complete change from feeling like she had to carry the weight. They married in the US but for a change of pace moved to the UK after a few years. They dedicated themselves to demanding work and travel schedules, both in the US and UK, moving every three or four years. Susan could always find marketing work locally and was able to build what she calls 'an eclectic but fantastic career'.

There were difficulties in the marriage, almost from the beginning, that she overlooked. Susan explains: 'He never took to stepfathering my children and didn't see the point of family time. He also didn't want to spend time getting to know my friends and neighbours. We became socially isolated. Those issues were brewing, but I wanted the marriage to work. I didn't want to go through another divorce.'

They both worked as consultants and once Susan overtook him on earnings, Thomas began to talk about his unfulfilled dream of working at a university.

She says: 'I was encouraging because you want your partner to be happy. Otherwise they can be absolutely miserable to be around! I didn't realise in the early days Thomas was never satisfied. His best job was always just around the corner. The ambition I'd always loved about him was now getting in the way of us settling down. I was really happy where we were in Liverpool.'

The last straw came just a few months after he moved to London, at what she thought was the last job. She remembers: 'He was in his early sixties by this point, at a reputable university, earning halfway decent money and in a city he'd always talked about. I was excited and thought we could finally settle down.'

Susan was commuting to London at weekends, as she was wrapping up her job in Liverpool. She was selling the house and preparing to move the family to London when Thomas announced he was being headhunted for another job in Stockholm.

She recalls: 'During the week I was on my own with the kids and starting to feel good about myself again. I was socialising with the friends it had taken me three years to get to know. When he announced this, I said, "But you just got there. . . and the rest of us are on our way to join you!" To which he replied, "Well, now I want to go to Stockholm."'

She continues: 'Hearing that made me realise *I'd had enough*. I honestly felt like I was choosing between life and death. I was so stressed I didn't recognise myself. I even suspected I might be menopausal, which it turned out I wasn't. I asked my daughter how she would feel if I left Thomas and she burst out crying, saying, "I've been waiting for you to say that for the last ten years."'

Unlike some of the other couples, Susan and Thomas's problems were not specifically related to her earnings but rather to his 'grass-is-always-greener' mentality. Susan felt his sense of responsibility decreased when he knew he could rely on her earnings and her consistent willingness to compromise. Like Stefano, Thomas enrolled in further education after they parted ways.

Susan also doesn't think her earning capability was a problem for the relationship, saying: 'He would have been delighted if I had always been the main earner, so he could do exactly what he wanted. I thought he was shirking some of his responsibilities. He had done this before. When he wanted to take a more rewarding, but less well-paid job, he couldn't understand his ex-wife's annoyance when he wanted to decrease her support payments. In the end I had to pick up the slack on his payments to her.'

Several other women mentioned being disgruntled at having to pay alimony or child support for their partner's children from a previous marriage.

In the case of Susan's first divorce, once he was working Stefano paid a nominal amount into a saving account for the children, but there was no settlement paid either way as she retained custody of the children. As for her second divorce, Susan is unsure if she will have to pay Thomas any maintenance but knows it is a real possibility.

Interestingly, Susan's second marriage helped shed light on what Stefano might have felt when they divorced. Susan says: 'I left Thomas because he was completely dominant. It was so liberating to realise that I could depend on myself. If it was like that for Stefano, he may have been thinking, *wow, my identity doesn't need to be wrapped up in Susan. I can make my own life now.*'

She explains a new realisation: 'I'm in my late forties and I have real opportunities now. My kids are gone, I'm no longer with my two husbands who earn less. I can now enjoy my earnings. I have never planned my career; latterly it's been based on where Thomas wanted to work. I gave up the ability to be strategic about which exact industry to be in or what type of experiences I wanted to have. Now I can build whatever career *I* want.

'What I now realise is that there is a part of me that became *less than*, and there's a part of my husbands that became *less than*. On your own you are forced to drive *yourself*.' She takes a deep breath when I ask, 'what next?' and she answers: 'That's the million dollar question! How do you reach your potential when you are just coasting? I honestly think there was an element of coasting on all our parts. It's too easy to give your power to somebody else.'

So, is the answer to have one person working flat-out, motivated, but mainly because others are reliant on them? Or would it be better if two people are both working at jobs they enjoy, but both coasting somewhat because they can both financially rely on each other? Perhaps it is a mix of both.

Susan answers: 'I think what worries me is becoming like my parents. They've been married 50 years. Mom stayed home and dad worked all day. What is sad is that each thought the other one had the easier deal.'

Men, like women, should be able to stay at home to maintain a household if it is what they love. The majority of women were clear they would not be good stay-at-home mothers. Whoever stays at home should do so because they are good at it, not to martyr themselves to the gendered sacrificial altar of 'motherhood'.

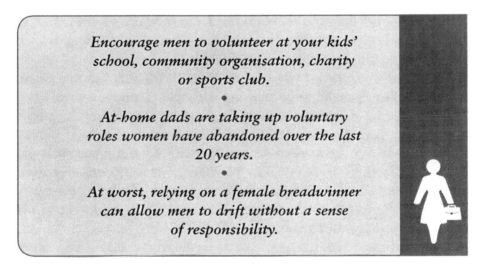

Encourage men to volunteer at your kids' school, community organisation, charity or sports club.

•

At-home dads are taking up voluntary roles women have abandoned over the last 20 years.

•

At worst, relying on a female breadwinner can allow men to drift without a sense of responsibility.

COMPROMISE MAKES A PARTNERSHIP

As anyone who is married or in a significant partnership knows, compromise and negotiation is the name of the game. You just cannot have a healthy, successful relationship without compromising, usually dozens of times each day. Negotiations can cover everything from who is picking up the children from school, holiday plans, which bills get priority, how to handle a misbehaving child to what you'll even eat for dinner. They are ongoing and require flexibility from both partners.

When one partner in a couple is the main breadwinner, the other partner is usually the one to compromise on their own career. Historically, this has been women who compromise on their career aspirations and personal time for the benefit of their husbands and children. To their credit, I now discovered many men who had compromised their own career choices or desires to do what worked best for their families and the high-earning wives who supported them.

Undoubtedly, discussions around female breadwinning historically focus on the 'saintly' men who compromise to take on traditionally female responsibilities. I know more than one client who has lamented how men in her office who leave early to take care of sick children are considered heroic by others, compared to the women in the office whose 'commitment' is questioned when they do the same thing.

However, several women I spoke with felt they did more than their fair share of compromising with their husbands, even when it would have made the most financial sense to follow *her* needs as the main breadwinner. Lisa and Malcolm are one such couple. They have been married for six years. Lisa has a fifteen-year-old son, Peter, from a previous marriage. Having previously lived in London, she moved with her son to Malcolm's hometown of Bristol after they married. This was the first of several big compromises Lisa made. It would not be her biggest.

For the first two years of their marriage they had earned equally, but for the last four years Lisa who is a solicitor, worked in a lucrative contract role where she brought home five times Malcolm's income. The job, however, was in Manchester. Lisa commuted weekly on the agreement that if she liked the role, the family would relocate to Manchester.

She remembers: 'When we were discussing it, Malcolm said he never wanted to stand between me and a job I wanted. I now know he wanted *me* to come to the realisation that staying in Bristol was best for all of us. He didn't want to follow me to Manchester, though he originally said he was open to relocating.'

Lisa had taken the initial risk in moving to Bristol, but Malcolm was not willing to make the same compromise for her job several years later. With a great dose of British understatement, Lisa says: 'If I'm honest, I became quite annoyed. I felt like I was living a double life travelling up and down the country each week. But four years into the job I realised Malcolm was never going to move, despite what he said. I had to think about what was more important: my job or my marriage. I really liked the job and if he'd been willing to come, I know I would've still been there. But after the four years, my enjoyment paled against the impact it was having on us. I realised I needed to make the compromise again.'

She now earns roughly half the family income as a solicitor in a local firm in Bristol. Lisa remarked that her first husband, Neil, was threatened by her success, so it is understandable that this experience weighed heavily on her mind when she had to make her decision. She was clearly wary of repeating what she perceived to be past mistakes.

To add to her stress, her son Peter also questioned why she would want to '*leave me and Malcolm*'. He was a weekly boarder at a fee-paying school he loved in Bristol, but made it clear he expected her to be nearby. Lisa says with some resentment: 'I know it was definitely not the norm, but lots of *men* work away during the week, and no one questions it. Why shouldn't women? Certainly the men I worked with made comments about our "odd" arrangement, even though they also worked away from home!

'It was my female colleagues who were more understanding. They saw how tough it was for me to balance both. The women were much more sensitive to the fact that it might have an impact on *me*, rather than just how difficult it must be for Malcolm and Peter.'

Friends and family were not very sympathetic either, always encouraging Lisa to give up her job in Manchester. She remembers: 'They'd say, "just come home," as if it was an easy decision. Once, when I was a bit fed up with all their "encouragement" to go back to Bristol *for the sake of the family*, I told my sister and her husband how much I earned and how dependent we all were on my income. They were shocked, saying, "That's more than our salaries combined!" Even then, they still felt I should return home.'

Notably, Lisa doesn't think anyone encouraged Malcolm to follow *her* to Manchester *for the sake of the family*. I suspect people worry more about 'the sake of the family' when it is a *woman* working away to earn that type of money. Men who work away from home are often seen as stalwart providers. While it may not be deemed healthy for family life, the really vehement opposition is reserved for women, and particularly mothers, who choose to do the same.

Lisa remembers: 'It was only after I left that job that Malcolm truly opened up and told me he wanted to be the main provider. It surprised me since he's so progressive in other areas. I didn't think he'd be that type of guy. At the end of the day, I believe most men want that "provider" role.'

She sighs: 'I don't believe women can have it all. It just depends on what you are willing to compromise on and ultimately what you are willing to sacrifice.' When I ask her what she sacrificed, she says with some sadness: 'A job I loved, unfortunately. I went in thinking I could have it all…but now I'm not so sure.'

How has her decision to leave the lucrative role affected their relationship? She pauses thoughtfully and then answers: 'I think we are happier. I have to believe it was worth it. Malcolm has promised that the next time I want to take a job he will compromise and follow me. I think if I had to do it again, I would double-check he was actually happy. He wasn't as honest as he could have been. We joke about it now.'

In order to be seen as supportive, Malcolm lied about his willingness to relocate – which probably had far greater consequences than had he been truthful from the start. There is a sense in the relationship that Malcolm *owes* Lisa because of the big compromises she has made over location. Whether or not she will ever be able to collect remains to be seen.

ON YOUR MARK, GET SET, STOP! MARRIAGE IS NOT A COMPETITION

Clearly, part of what bothered Malcolm and indeed a few other men was the sense of unspoken competition they felt to be the main breadwinner.

Malcolm and Lisa were not alone in having a slim thread of

competition woven throughout the relationship. Based in Paris, Josephine and Pierre started out in their early twenties in the same industry: information technology. She worked as an IT trainer and he was on desktop support within the same company when they met.

She remembers with a sly grin: 'I spotted him at a coffee shop each morning, and decided to become a regular there myself, so I could bump into him. Considering I was no huge fan of coffee to begin with, I developed quite an espresso habit in addition to catching his eye.'

They have been married eight years and have two daughters. When asked what drew her to him, she says: 'He was just nice, a real change from many of my previous boyfriends who all had some sort of psychological dysfunction! Pierre was shyer than me and not as career-driven. He wasn't who I would have pictured myself with, but I was smart enough to notice him.'

Josephine and Pierre came from very different backgrounds. Pierre went to exclusive fee-paying schools and held an advanced IT qualification. Josephine was raised by her single mum who left school when she found herself alone and pregnant with Josephine in her late teens. She explains: 'My mother worked a full day job and then we would clean offices at night. I would help her in the evening and I have a photo of me when I was little holding a mop taller than I was, with a big smile on my face.'

She left school at sixteen to help support her mother. She learned all of her IT skills on the job and was able to work her way up. She says: 'I remember as a little girl looking to the tall buildings in Paris, and saying to my mum, "Someday I'm going to work in those towers and we are going to live in the countryside."' Understandably, Josephine's purchase of a house for her mother rates as one of her proudest accomplishments.

Josephine worked as an IT trainer for several years. Eventually, wanting more of a challenge, she moved into desktop support near Pierre. They progressed at the same rate and always with a hint of competition. She recalls: 'We did the same job in the same company for several years. One year he got a larger bonus than me, not by much, but we could never figure out exactly where it came from. I do remember resenting it though.'

Five years into their marriage, Josephine moved away from IT in technology firms and into IT in the oil and gas industry, which she saw as more lucrative. She explains: 'When I was on maternity leave, I was always looking to see what else was out there. One day I saw an IT role I could do for a petrochemical firm. I called to ask the manager if he would meet me for coffee, and after meeting me he offered me the job on the spot. It was still the lowest position on the food chain, but I wanted to move into an industry with more potential for growth.'

After Josephine's jump into the oil and gas industry she began to significantly out-earn Pierre. Ever ambitious, she worked her way rapidly up the ladder. She now brings home three quarters of the family's earnings. She explains: 'My significant increases are down to two things: I moved to a more lucrative industry and I have made a conscious decision to move every two years. You can always trade up more easily when you are jumping jobs. It would be nearly impossible for Pierre to catch me up now because each time I jump I earn 15,000–20,000 Euros more.'

When asked whether she saw her role as main breadwinner continuing, she automatically responds: 'I tell Pierre there is a chance he could catch me up but in reality it's very unlikely.'

Interestingly, not assuming their status as main breadwinner was permanent was one way women helped manage their partner's ego. This approach was taken even if it was a pattern over several years and the likelihood of it changing was highly improbable. The idea that their male partners could eventually be on a par with or even out-earn their wives seemed important to the maintenance of their equality.

When asked about her rationale for changing job so frequently, Josephine, who is 38, takes a very pragmatic approach: 'Two years is long enough to learn virtually everything you need to do that job. If a company hasn't developed you sufficiently in that time, they never will. Ultimately, I want to jump jobs every two years until I am 40, so that I can take my foot off the accelerator then and enjoy life a bit more knowing I have the role I want.'

She compares her career strategy to Pierre's: 'He likes an easier life and isn't as confident as I am. In fact, almost every promotion or job change he's made has come from my suggestion. Plus, because of his age, it would now be hard for him to move into a more lucrative industry since he doesn't have experience outside of IT.

'He talks about making a career move and knows he could probably earn more, but he doesn't push himself. He could tell his boss about his career goals or network like I do. If I suggest those things, he gets annoyed, so I don't. Instead I just focus on what I can do with *my own* career to benefit us all.'

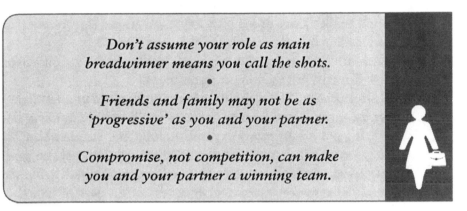

Don't assume your role as main breadwinner means you call the shots.

•

Friends and family may not be as 'progressive' as you and your partner.

•

Compromise, not competition, can make you and your partner a winning team.

'CAN'T YOU TAKE A JOKE?'
HOW HOSTILITY REARS ITS HEAD

Joking is a seemingly safe way to vent tensions, and is a method several couples used to cope with any resentment regarding non-traditional gender roles.

When asked how Josephine's being the primary breadwinner has affected the relationship, she sighs: 'He is very proud of me and a great source of support. Pierre *says* he is absolutely fine with it, but I think there is a bit of personal disappointment for him. He often makes jokes at his own expense.' It was this *joking* that was a familiar theme for many of the women.

Jokes often stem from a grain of truth which is difficult to express directly, but may mask resentment.

She elaborates: 'The night after I was recognised at an industry dinner, he complained he was "always the bridesmaid, never the bride". It's not a joke at my expense exactly, but it does show his resentment. When I told him about being headhunted, he said, "Pretty soon you'll be able to piss standing up!" which made me laugh at the time – but again it shows there's a part of him that isn't completely comfortable with the strides I've made.'

The fact that Pierre uses self-deprecation, and very gendered language, to joke speaks to his difficulty with the blurring of boundaries between their roles. She explained: 'Pierre would never joke about my earnings in front of other people, as I know he would prefer other people to think we are equivalent earners.'

Josephine and Pierre are not alone in using humour to vent any tension. Vashti earns 60 per cent of the household earnings through her work as a security specialist. When discussing her husband's feelings about their income gap, she says with some uncertainty: 'I don't think it's a big issue for Terence. But I do think it galls him slightly that he works so many more hours than I do. When I think about it, I've just been lucky falling into a well-paid industry.'

While we talk about any resentment Terence may feel, her tone is somewhat tentative as if she is unsure *just how much* it actually bothers him.

Vashti frequently uses the word *lucky* to describe her career, which in my opinion diminishes the savvy choices she has made. She has clearly made a few astute decisions to reach the senior level she has attained. I suspect describing herself as *lucky* to others helps her feel less 'calculating' which is a concern for many professional women. It's probably a more comfortable way to describe her success when comparing it to that of her husband whom she clearly loves and respects.

When asked how she knows it 'galls him a bit', Vashti explains: 'Every now and again he breaks down what I earn on a per hour basis to show the huge difference between us; but it's always said in a joking way.' She elaborates: 'He thinks I work less hard, and it annoys him slightly. He'll say you don't need to be terribly clever to make a good living in airline security, given it's a boom industry since 9/11.'

When asked if she ever *jokes back* to defend herself, she laughs and says: 'If he's goading me I will say, "I chose this career and I work fewer hours than you, making more money than you...so who's the clever one?" – but that's usually after a few cocktails!'

She becomes much more serious and says more thoughtfully: 'I am incredibly conscious of it, and I do think there is an esteem issue there for men. They want to show they are in control to the external world.' As an example, Vashti says: 'I will slightly downplay my bonuses, unless I know he has had a great year himself, just to be sensitive.'

Signs Your Partner May Not Be Suited to Secondary Breadwinner Status:

He's competitive and raises his own goals with every achievement you make.

•

He minimises your accomplishments through hostile jokes or even open aggression.

•

He cites the negative things other people think about your relationship.

•

He undermines your efforts by being passive-aggressive and routinely 'forgetting' to do tasks.

•

He spends his own money but doesn't think he should contribute to the pot if he earns less.

•

He openly flirts with other women or has affairs to boost his own sense of self-confidence.

•

He believes children are better off with their mother at home.

Signs You May Not Be Cut Out to Be a Female Breadwinner:

You secretly hope your future husband will earn more, and seek out men in high-earning fields.

•

You have always dreamed of staying at home with your children.

•

You believe in a fairly traditional division of tasks at home.

•

You view expensive gifts as an integral part of any relationship.

•

Your husband's profession is part of how you define your own success.

8

DIRTY, SEXY MONEY

'I make money using my brains and lose money listening to my heart. But in the long run my books balance pretty well.'

KATE SEREDY
The Singing Tree

As you would expect from an exploration of female breadwinning, money is never far from the surface of any issue. Women are both individually and collectively earning more than ever before which quite understandably creates a shift in the power dynamic amongst most couples. This is hugely important as money represents what we value and sheds light on our belief system. I am a great fan of the adage *if you want to know what people truly value, look at what how they spend their time and money.*

Most couples argue about finance from time to time, regardless of where the money comes from. In fact, a recent study found 72 per cent of young professional couples have argued about money at some point. Impending marriage does nothing to encourage greater communication on the topic. In fact, most couples (91 per cent) avoid talking about finances and less than half (43 per cent) talked about their attitudes towards money before they married.[101]

In the same study, one third of couples said finances were the

---

[101] American Express Saving and Spending Tracker, June 10, 2010

main stressor in their relationship, ahead of intimacy, children and in-laws. Such was the level of financial secrecy that many were more sure of their partner's weight than their salary.

However, times may be changing as *young* professional couples were almost twice as likely (81 per cent) to talk about money as the couples from the general population (43 per cent).

MONEY'S TOO TIGHT TO MENTION

And talk they must. Couples who argue about money once a week are 30 per cent more likely to divorce than those who disagree about money just once a month.[102] The management of money remains one of the top reasons why couples part ways.

However, the way a couple approaches saving, spending and investing can actually be points of bonding and affection. If you create and accomplish a shared goal, a wedding, a deposit for a first home or retirement savings, it can be a huge boost for a relationship. This shared goal enables both partners to feel respected and cared for.

It will also help you get to know your partner better. Our attitudes towards money are a direct reflection of or reaction to the way we were raised. Therapists term money a 'family of origin' issue; understanding your partner's attitudes will underscore how they grew up and how their parents treated money.

Like the husbands of many of the women we will discuss in this chapter, Simon manages the family's expenditure. In fact, a majority of women I met delegated day-to-day control of family financial planning and even investment decisions to their husbands. As Simon's wife, Katrina, says: 'I couldn't tell you how much I made last year. Simon and I talk about our finances, but I don't know how much is in our accounts on a day-to-day basis.'

Katrina and Simon are equally happy with the arrangement and

---

[102] Amato and Rogers (1997) Jeffrey P Dew 'Financial issues as predictors of divorce', Paper presented at the annual conference of the National Council on Family Relations (November 2009), San Francisco, CA

see it continuing until Katrina retires. She explains: 'We are both conscientious savers. If anything, he pushes me to spend more on myself. He actually finds it funny. He says, "If they averaged your salary over every hour you give, your boss probably gets a great deal!" But we don't get carried away by the amounts I earn because we both know the party could be over tomorrow. In fact, we may come to a point where we *want* it to be over tomorrow.'

The trust she feels for his money management skills is vital.

Perceptions of how well one's spouse handles money plays a role in shaping the quality and stability of family life. Individuals who feel their spouses handle money poorly are less happy in their marriages.[103] In fact, in one study, feeling that one's spouse spent money foolishly increased the likelihood of divorce by 45 per cent for both men and women. Only extramarital affairs and substance abuse are stronger predictors of divorce.[104]

Not surprisingly, couples who avoided money talk often had problematic relationships.

MONEY... THE DISCUSSION THAT NEVER HAPPENS

While Annie's husband Graham has been in full-time employment for most of their marriage, Annie, a documentary film maker, now brings home 95 per cent of the household income while he invests in his start-up.

How would she react if Graham earned more than her? She exclaims: 'That would be fantastic! We could pay off the mortgage! I do feel the business has to be successful in some way, otherwise he has been living off me for several years.' The way she phrases it is telling – but does Graham feel that same obligation? She sighs: 'It's the biggest discussion we *don't* have. If we have a row about anything, money's the one area we avoid. It's too problematic to be honest.'

---

[103] Britt, S, Grable, J, Nelson-Goff, B, White, M (2008) 'The influence of perceived spending behaviors on relationship satisfaction', *Financial Counseling and Planning*, 19, 31–43
[104] Amato, P & Rogers, S (1997) 'A longitudinal study of marital problems and subsequent divorce', *Journal of Marriage and the Family*, 59, 612–624

Annie says she and Graham don't argue about money specifically, but about *time* as an issue. The unspoken assumption is that her time is more *monetarily* valuable than his. She explains: 'The other day we had an argument about him accompanying me to a parent-teacher night a few weeks ago. He didn't want to go, saying he didn't have time. I said that we both needed to go and that if *I* could make time, then *he* could make time.'

Annie admits that some of the problem is in how she views his daily schedule.

She explains: 'Graham works from home, so I see that as an opportunity to do a few personal things too, because they are far easier to do in that setting. I travel frequently, and am rarely in the studio.'

Speaking as someone who also works from home, I will concede that it is far easier to make personal calls on behalf of the family. She continues: 'When I ask him to call British Gas, he complains and asks why I can't call them myself. I manage the nanny, all the children's schooling and doctor's appointments. When I ask him to do something, he gets annoyed but I don't shout, "You know I can't call them because I am working to bring in the money!"'

As much as they dance around the issue of her job versus his, that issue remains. Annie says: 'I may never say anything explicitly, but he's said to me, "I hate when you allude to the money," which shows that we are both aware of it. No matter how I think I am brushing it under the rug, it's there.'

How does Annie reconcile that, from a purely financial standpoint, her time *is* more valuable than his? She sighs: 'In the end, I call British Gas myself. It's easier for everyone if I just do it. If you have children, I think it tends to be the woman who takes care of things. If I am working at the weekend, I have to remind him about the children's mealtimes. I console myself knowing that it seems to be that way for all my other girlfriends as well. In fact, of all the other female partners I work with, we are *all* the main breadwinners and we do the majority of household stuff too.'

I notice that the women who had problems with their partners taking on greater domestic responsibility are also those who argue that 'women can't have it all' or that all other female breadwinners are 'in the same boat'.

What I have discovered is that female breadwinners are *not* all in the same boat. Many have husbands and partners who do step up to take on housework and childcare. I think the belief that *all other women* face such challenges helps them accept the reluctance of the men in their lives to take on what it means to be a *partner*.

Interestingly, Annie and Graham do talk around the topic when discussing what they see in *other* couples. She says: 'We recently had lunch with some friends. While the wife is very successful, her husband has been in and out of work and then went back for a postgraduate degree. During the meal, she was quite dismissive of his course and openly said, "I never thought I'd be in my forties with my husband as a full-time student!" which was kind of difficult to witness.

'On the drive back, Graham brought it up saying it couldn't have been easy for her husband to face several redundancies and be back in university so late in life, with a wife who was questioning him.' Being publicly chided about the disparity in their careers could not have been pleasant for the husband to hear or for them to witness, but it allowed Annie and Graham the opportunity to discuss their situation in an *indirect* way.

Like other women I spoke with, Annie mentioned that it would be interesting to hear what her partner thought of the arrangement. Interestingly, it was often the women who *didn't* talk through the issue with their partners who were most curious as to how their partners would have responded to being interviewed. Perhaps, again, the interview on the topic would have forced an issue they were avoiding.

Explaining why they avoid talking about money, Annie says: 'If you open up that can of worms, you can never go back. My way of dealing with it is to avoid bringing it up. I know that if I forced the issue, about him contributing more with the children for example, it could get ugly. I remind the friends who give me a hard time about him that it's *our* money. If I looked at it like *his* or *my* money, we'd have a lot more trouble. Some of them do think it's a weird arrangement and that he's taking advantage of the situation by living off me but *not* being a stay-at-home dad.'

It is interesting that for Annie and Graham, as well as other couples, it is the taking on of the domestic role of being a stay-at-home dad that gives the arrangement validity and moral weight. She recognises the hypocrisy of how high-earning senior men with stay-at-home wives are never questioned. However, I would also say that the prevalence of even this arrangement is rapidly diminishing; there is an increasing sense that work of some kind, *and* childcare, is expected for both women and men.

Annie is philosophical about how the *amount* of money in question affects the issue: 'The more you earn, the less it matters if your partner earns very little. When I was married to my first husband, Jonathan, neither of us were high earners, so I resented that he wasn't contributing in any way. I felt the pennies more. Now, I earn enough so that Graham, the kids and I are secure. I'm probably also more confident in who I am as a person now that I am in my forties, especially compared to who I was in my twenties!'

This comment reminded me of how Daphne regarded Adrian's low earnings. Even if in full-time work, his lack of qualifications would mean his pay would be so low it would be insignificant to the couple. Money had ceased to be the real issue for them. It was more convenient for both of them for him to be at home. Money mattered less to her *because* she was such a high earner. The *value* they both derived from him taking care of daily life and being able to travel according to her hectic work schedule outweighed the minimal financial contribution he might be able to offer.

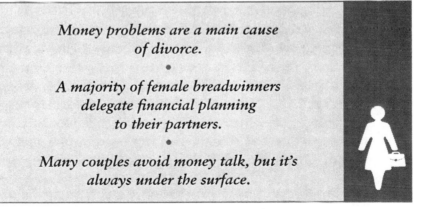

Money problems are a main cause of divorce.

•

A majority of female breadwinners delegate financial planning to their partners.

•

Many couples avoid money talk, but it's always under the surface.

CONTROLLING THE PURSE STRINGS

One might expect the person holding the purse strings in the relationship to hold the power. Others might assume the earner makes the major purchasing decisions and controls day-to-day spending. However, when asked about how their family managed money, the female breadwinners I spoke to turned this theory on its head.

Instead of consolidating the power of their earnings to use as a tool in the relationship, these women take a much more equitable approach to money. They share financial information, are likely to delegate money management and exercise joint decision-making. For them, the person who controls the day-to-day financial management should be the person who is more competent at the task – not necessarily the earner of the money.

Annie, a documentary film maker, cringes at the memory of her own mother's financial reliance on her father. She remembers her asking Annie's father for extra housekeeping money to buy underwear.

That memory had a massive impact on Annie. She vowed to never be dependent on a man: 'I always knew I would earn as much or more than any husband I had. From my first day out of film school, I just knew I wanted to make groundbreaking documentaries. I never thought about how my earning would affect the relationship.'

Annie is the only woman I interviewed who ever anticipated that she might out-earn a future husband.

While women on the whole took pains to introduce their partners to the responsibilities of financial planning, there was some truth to the phrase the power of the purse. One US study found that 65 per cent of women consider themselves their family's chief financial planner, and 71 per cent called themselves the family accountant.[105] In some cases, the female breadwinners did control financial planning but it was not a task most of them relished. There was certainly no sense that the women used

---

[105] GfK Roper for NBC Universal (2009) 'The Female Factor'

financial planning as any type of weapon, and even the ones who managed the money said they would be happier if their partner took an interest in the family finances.

Carly, a research scientist, clearly falls into this category. She admits: 'It sounds dreadful, but if I gave him control, I'm not sure if we'd be in as good a position as we are. If I do it, I know the bills are paid and how much we have in the current account. He's not exactly frivolous, but I don't think he would be on top of it, so at least this way I know it gets done.'

Bill and Maureen have a joint account for household expenses as well as separate accounts. She says: 'He once accused me of being a control freak about the money, saying I needed to be in charge. I told him I'd love him to take it over, yet he still did nothing about it. It wasn't a real grievance; it was just something to throw at me in the heat of an argument.'

She organises all their investments, as he is dubious about investments or property. Frustratingly for Maureen, Bill doesn't save any of the money he brings in through freelance writing towards his retirement. He eschews any conversations with Maureen about retirement planning, as he says he can't imagine a day when he won't work. On his quieter days, however, he openly talks about what he'd like to do when he retires. This disconnect between *earning and saving* money causes real tension in many couples, no matter who brings home the bacon.

Interestingly, whilst I did not look specifically at spending patterns, a SheSpeaks 2009 survey found that female breadwinners made purchasing decisions differently from unemployed married women. While female breadwinners were more stressed about the economy compared to non-working women (47 per cent compared with 34 per cent), they were also more willing to spend discretionary income.

They were also less likely to seek spousal recommendation before purchasing a big-ticket item such as electronics or a car. Instead, they prefer to rely on a wider network of family and friends for recommendations.[106] The female breadwinners I spoke

---

[106] SheSpeaks (2010) 'Spending in Uncertain Times' www.shespeaks.com/recessionshopping

with certainly did mention the freedom of not having to ask permission to make big purchases, although virtually all of them said they shared decisions for major items.

HE'S THE BANKER:
LETTING HIM HANDLE THE MONEY

In reality, traditional resource theory which suggests that the earner holds the power simply doesn't hold true for most of these relationships. For the first time in history, female breadwinners are in the position of *choosing* equality with their husbands, rather than hoping equality is *given* to them.

So, why are women, who could quite rightly choose to control the purse strings as generations of male breadwinners have historically done, so generous in exercising financial equality?

Interestingly, Merryn Somerset-Webb, editor of *MoneyWeek* magazine and author of *Love is Not Enough,* noticed the same tendencies in the way female breadwinners manage money with their partners. In terms of day-to-day money management, there was a trend for *all* money to be fed into a joint account and then bills to be paid from there. If this could be argued to be a more egalitarian model, why do women take such pains to be fair with the money?

Merryn smiles: 'I think women don't want to be seen as "controlling". She already has the more senior career, and perhaps doesn't want her husband to feel any sense of inferiority. There must never be any sense he is *taking* money from her. Women believe that will impact his ego and damage their relationship.'

She continues: 'Certainly, if you listen to all the scaremongers in the media who say progressive women are making modern men redundant, then that is a legitimate fear.' Indeed, a disproportionate number of women, even if they paid bills directly from their own accounts, often let their partners manage the investments and longer-term financial planning. In fact, several said they had no direct dealings with money management at all, preferring to leave it to their partners.

For example, Jacques handles all of the family investments and financial administration. Anita, a sales executive, says: 'We got into the habit when we were living in France and he could more easily read the paperwork. The habit stuck and now I just come home in the evening, and he's left papers on my desk to sign. Occasionally, when we have a big argument, I worry that I should understand better where the money is going. At the end of the day, though, I trust him 100 per cent. It's probably a nice way of him feeling like he's in control too, that he has as much say over the money as I do.'

Melanie, who works in the automotive industry, also allows Connor to manage all of their money. She exclaims: 'I'm terrible. I have no idea about the money. He goes online and ferries it between our various saving and spending accounts. I don't have the first clue. I never look at the statements. He uses our joint account for bills and all his own spending.' When I ask Melanie, who seems quite happy in the arrangement, if Connor has ever shown any resentment about not having his own pot of money, she quickly replies: 'Never! It doesn't bother him in the least. It's just where we keep all our spending money.'

Why have they chosen this model? She answers: 'It's probably a reaction to the way I was brought up. My father earned the money and gave my mum a small allowance. She had to ask for every little extra thing we needed. He controlled her through that account. I never wanted Connor to feel so powerless. Besides, he enjoys working with numbers and I don't. It made the decision rather easy for us.'

Several of the female breadwinners I met were not married to their long-time partners. Interestingly, they themselves said they would feel vulnerable if they were financially dependent on a man but not married. As dubious a security net as being legally wed is, it does provide far better for a partner, in the event of an untimely death, than no contract. Because over the last 50 years, so much publicity has been given to the economic plight of women whose partners leave, women may be more acutely aware of the dangers of being so dependent on someone, yet unmarried.

However, the men with whom they lived were not concerned

about the potential precariousness of their situation. In these unmarried partnerships perhaps the men do not think of *themselves* as dependent, even if realistically a break-up would create a serious decline in their standard of living.

Daphne remarks: 'If I was Adrian I'd feel much more exposed. I think perhaps he feels untouchable. I have said many times that we should just make it official and get married, but he can't see the point after fifteen years together.'

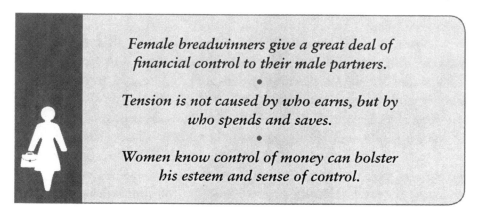

Female breadwinners give a great deal of financial control to their male partners.

•

Tension is not caused by who earns, but by who spends and saves.

•

Women know control of money can bolster his esteem and sense of control.

SPENDING ON HIS OWN TERMS

Needless to say, money and its utility was an issue for several of the couples. We will be discussing more on how couples successfully handled money later on, but I noticed a pattern in some men's attitudes towards joint money. To a few men, it wasn't joint at all. They only felt entitled to spend what was truly theirs, even when this paled next to their partner's earnings.

To this end, several men in the couples I met were very clear in spending only what they earned, not touching their high-earning partner's salary. Obviously this worked more in principle than in reality, as the women were likely to pay for mortgages and bills, the benefits of which they would both enjoy.

For example, Josephine, whose husband also works full-time, manages all investments, bills and even the cash – but the couple keep two separate accounts. 'We have never looked at it as "my money" or "his money". We spend it as we see fit, and regularly top up each other's account. Pierre is much more cautious and doesn't spend a lot, probably only spending what he brings in. He reels me in when I need it. When you look at his bank statement, it's all petrol bills, groceries and mortgage. He jokes that he needs to get a life.'

She continues: 'In addition to our other bills, my statements are full of restaurant bills, drinks out, clothes for the kids, shoes at Gucci. He jokes, "You're living *la vida loca*, aren't you?" I do like my bags and shoes, and making sure our girls have what they need. If he has a go at me, I will remind him with a laugh, "I'm an overall profit centre, not a cost centre." If it is a serious money decision we will always talk it out though, and I do *give in* to him more than I might do so that he knows he has a say.'

Similarly, Daphne's partner, Adrian, is not particularly driven by her salary. Daphne says: 'He's not interested in the money. Of course, I point out that he is interested in what the money brings – our memberships to the gym and two golf clubs. He also loves to travel, and I am past the age of wanting to do it on the cheap, so he does benefit. But he doesn't spend much and it's never been a concern that he's with me for the money.'

Maureen's husband, Bill, also spends on his own terms, which causes resentment in the relationship. She explains: 'Once he contributes from his earnings to our joint pot, he's thinks he's "done". I pay for all the food, petrol, family holidays, anything for Sarah, out of my separate account. He will occasionally buy a few bits from the grocery store, but never what we need for dinner. A few years ago, he even went through a stage when he would tell me how much he had spent as if I was supposed to reimburse him!'

Maria experienced a similar impasse with her partner, Elliott. Maria says: 'I don't think the difference in our salaries bothers him too much. I think Elliott is unusual, in that he spends like someone who earns £50,000 a year, not like someone whose wife also brings in £300,000 a year. He probably thinks I place too much importance on money.

'Last year we went to France. I didn't book our villa early

enough so I had to pay a lot when I eventually remembered. Elliott will sarcastically say, "Money can't solve all our problems and if you think ahead we wouldn't pay so much."' Interestingly, the idea of organising the accommodation himself was not raised.

She continues: 'Likewise, we had ongoing problems with the electrics in our house which he couldn't fix. Finally, I called out the electricians, the best and most expensive in the area. He was so annoyed and said, "You can't always just throw money at a problem, Maria. It doesn't always fix everything." When he says that, I see a thread of resentment. It's a tension that is not normally there. He's not cheap, and he encourages me to spend money on myself and the children, but he won't do it for himself.'

Maria says: 'Fundamentally, there is nothing he wants that money can buy. So, for example, I like to have expensive holidays, but he prefers to go camping and ride his motorbike.'

As we are talking, it seems to me that the distinguishing factor between when Elliott encourages or chastises Maria for spending money is when money is a tool *she* can use to solve a problem quickly. It is a tool he feels he does not have, and one that supersedes his own tool of choice, brain power. To my suggestion of this pattern, Maria agrees: 'Yes, that's it exactly.' She jokes: 'But when he is sarcastic, I say back to him, "Well, I don't need to *think*; I've got *money*!"'

Maria and Elliott, like many others I talked with, have individual accounts and investments. Elliott works full-time and could save money but chooses not to. She explains: 'I want to talk to him about our investments. He'll say, "I don't know why you worry, you have so much money you couldn't even spend it all." Then he'll point out that he barely pays into his work pension.'

This is particularly salient because the couple are not married and Elliott would not automatically inherit her pension if she suddenly died. He has been clear with her that he wants her will to name only the children as beneficiaries.

To help rectify this, Maria has offered many times to set up a joint account but says that Elliott refuses: 'He doesn't want my money. It's a matter of honour. It's probably a sign to himself that he can live without me. He wants to show me he doesn't need it. I think he doesn't want to give up an aspect of his manhood.'

Money in exchange for masculinity is a theme felt by several of the couples. The underlying assumption may be 'if I take my partner's money, then I'm accepting I *need* my partner's money.' Maria says, however: 'I suspect, if he earned double tomorrow, he would spend more. He certainly enjoys good wine, our nice cars, our lavish holidays. But he likes to tell me and *himself* that he doesn't need them and he's as happy without.'

So, how would she feel if he earned more? 'I'd love it! If he was earning more money, it would give me options I've never had – like leaving my job. I'd love to do something entrepreneurial. So perhaps there will always be a bit of resentment in me because I can never rely on him that way.'

THE DEVASTATION OF DEBT

For some couples, having the husband who earns less manage the family finances clearly works. The women hand over their pay packet, so to speak, and trust their partners to manage it responsibly. We will look at how to make it work even better in the next chapter.

Most men treat that trust with the high esteem it deserves. For others, failure to talk about money can lead to complete disaster. This was heartbreakingly illustrated when I met Kirstie, a senior IT manager.

Kirstie and Giles have been married for five years, but were together before their marriage for an additional nine years. When they met, Giles was an IT contractor and earning more than Kirstie. She had just joined the same organisation as a permanent employee.

Giles was very encouraging of her career in the early days, but she laughs: 'It was only when I became senior that he mysteriously became less supportive!' By the time they married, Kirstie was earning significantly more, and she continues to bring home the vast majority of their joint income.

As Kirstie was climbing the ladder to her managerial role, Giles, an engineer, became increasingly jealous and even dismissive of her success. She says: 'When we met, he said he liked strong women. That was until he married one!'

The tension was added to in that she couldn't tell him about certain issues she was privy to at work. Earlier on, she had confided in him about an impending restructuring. He told his colleagues about the imminent changes, breaking her trust in him. As an understandable reaction, she stopped sharing confidential issues with him.

Meanwhile, she continued to get plaudits about the job she was doing. The fact that they worked together meant her success was all the more visible to Giles, and perhaps acted as salt to his growing wound. After they married, Giles mysteriously became so depressed that he was prescribed medication. Kirstie could not pinpoint what was changing. Their relationship suffered dramatically. She says: 'He wouldn't tell me what was going on at first. We were now working in the same large directorate and he was reporting to a manager, who reported to another person, who then reported to *me*. Colleagues were making fun of him that he was "working for his wife".

'I don't think in a hierarchical way, so even though I was technically senior to him as a contractor, I never thought about it like that. I didn't realise other people weren't quite so egalitarian in their thinking!'

She continues: 'He wasn't strong enough to brush it off, let alone defend my success. Instead, he would accuse me of being too controlling and *treating him like one of my minions*, which really hurt.'

To make matters worse, Kirstie's own boss became much more difficult and demanding, bullying and deriding her in public. Kirstie felt that she couldn't talk about work at home, nor could she open up to friends at work about the issues she was having with Giles.

As the relationship deteriorated, the original source of Giles's depression was revealed. He was maintaining a debt of over £100,000 and was in danger of losing their house, a secret he hid from her while they were living together.

He had reassured her that he would always send off all the

bill payments, since he had historically earned more and would intercept the post from her.

As an IT contractor, Giles worked for a several companies that defaulted on their payments to him. He didn't tell Kirstie, instead hiding bank statements before she could see them. He proceeded to spend money as if everything was normal. This no doubt increased his stress every day. After he finally confessed to the debt, Giles quit work and filed for bankruptcy.

While the fault clearly lies with Giles for hiding the debt, Kirstie had never asked to look at bank statements or create a joint account. Because Giles was such a high earner she felt she had no need to worry. She says: 'Money was just one of those things you don't talk about. I tried to keep him sweet by not questioning him.' She speaks slowly: 'The long-term consequences of that approach have been devastating. We should have had a joint account from the start.'

Additionally, while Giles must have always been somewhat insecure, his jealousy increased after they married. Kirstie remembers: 'He'd say, "Why do you have to spend so much time with Jerry in your team? You'd rather be with them than with me."' She had hoped their marriage would allay his jealousy and depression.

The pressure mounted on Kirstie, as she was now the sole breadwinner and responsible for a man who she says: '...was so angry, he would go weeks at a time without speaking to me.' After many months, eventually Kirstie crumbled. She said: 'I came home after work one day, and I couldn't stop crying. I went to bed and didn't get out for a week. I had tried to keep work and home completely separate, but it just wasn't possible.'

She explains her next steps: 'I had to talk to someone, as I had become completely isolated. After my breakdown, I thought, *what the hell am I doing? You can either become a broken person or you can fight back.* I told Giles about the bullying at work and insisted that we get marriage counselling. He agreed to the idea because he thought it would "fix" me. He blamed all our problems on my job. After several sessions, the counsellor pointed out that while I had indeed begun to push back on my boss, Giles was taking no responsibility for the way he was treating me in our home life. He ignored me for weeks on end and was being completely ungrateful that my pay packet allowed him a way out of bankruptcy.'

So, did the counsellor's observation give him the perspective he needed? Kirstie laughs: 'He was livid! He accused me of being married to my job and told me these were all *my* issues. He walked out of therapy and never went back. But the key thing was that *I* continued to go to counselling on my own. It was a lifeline. It gave me the tools I needed to be able to cope. I had to build up my confidence again and not lower myself to Giles's level.

'I learned to ignore it if he tried to pick a fight. There is nothing to win from arguing. If you score the point, your husband feels belittled. If you give in for the sake of a quieter life, you lose a piece of yourself.' She continues: 'I don't waste my time any more trying to pacify him. Refusing to argue helps keep me sane. Fighting back only feeds his anger and makes him feel he's been legitimately wronged. I'm his wife, not his mother. He has to grow up.' Kirstie stuck it out through what could only be described as several hellish first years of marriage.

The fact that the problems intensified right after their marriage suggests the legalising of their relationship had forced Giles to address his expectations of what it means to be a good provider. Being secretly deep in debt while his new wife was comfortably out-earning him may have shed a less than favourable light on how he was dealing with those roles. Kirstie reflects: 'He's never been hugely confident, and I think he felt a self-imposed pressure to be *the husband*.'

When I listen to Kirstie's story, I am amazed she could stay with a man who alternated between spewing bitter comments and ignoring her completely for several years. How did she manage? She sighs: 'I considered leaving many times, but I knew he couldn't manage on his own. He had no job or money and I didn't want to make him homeless as well.' She takes on a very care-giving role and Giles benefited from what some would say was unwarranted generosity on her part.

I am struck with wonder that they even made it to five years of marriage. She explains: 'He began to thaw as time went on. He realised I would stand by him, help him through bankruptcy and that I was willing to be his partner. Even though I earned so much more money, I never used it as a weapon against him. We were in this together. But his acceptance of me has only come about in the last year or so.'

It is almost as if Giles expected Kirstie to leave, and baited her continually to drive her away.

As a coach, it seems to me that Giles began to open up to Kirstie again when she showed him the unconditional acceptance he could not show himself. It could not have been easy for him to hold on to such bitterness for so many years, particularly when he was clearly at fault over the hidden debt and subsequent treatment of his wife. Kirstie's acceptance of him meant Giles could accept himself.

At this suggestion, Kirstie agrees and says: 'I don't think Giles likes himself very much, and the counsellor said he needed to find a better outlet for his anger than me. He does need to cope better and he doesn't do anything to help himself. He drinks and smokes, and avoids all forms of exercise. I have to exercise and watch what I eat to stay on top of things.'

Crucially, other men have commented on how lucky Giles was, which has helped heal their relationship. A good friend went through bankruptcy and lost his home and family as a result. He pointed out to Giles that Kirstie was the sole reason he was able to live the kind of leisurely life he could now, taking on contract work and generally being a house husband. Kirstie suspects this comment from another *man* probably helped put things in perspective for him.

Ironically, Giles's own father left his wife with a great amount of debt and a house in foreclosure when Giles was a child. This huge shock forced his mother to spend most days and evenings working to provide for him and his brother. Rather than take out his anger on his father, even as an adult Giles has never forgiven his *mother* for not being there for him while she was working. In particular, he blamed her for moving in with another man when Giles's younger brother, Malcolm, was fifteen.

Kirstie reflects: 'I think she just needed a life of her own by then. She was married and pregnant with Giles by the time she was nineteen. She never had a chance at happiness on her own. Giles and his father never talked about what happened and he never held his father responsible for abandoning the family. Perhaps not surprisingly, Kirstie is closer to her mother-in-law than Giles is, maybe out of a mutual respect and recognition for the way they have both taken care of Giles.

The couple would like to move house, but Giles cannot co-sign another mortgage, so the house move would be totally her responsibility. Does she ever resent Giles for the situation they are in? She sighs and says: 'Yes, I do. Mostly because I feel tired and daunted. I want to leave my job, but I wonder how I can maintain this precarious balance we have now. A new job would mean me spending two or three nights a week on the road.

'Sometimes I just wish I could do what he does, playing on a computer with no real responsibility.'

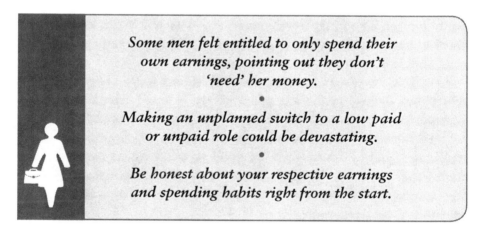

Some men felt entitled to only spend their own earnings, pointing out they don't 'need' her money.

•

Making an unplanned switch to a low paid or unpaid role could be devastating.

•

Be honest about your respective earnings and spending habits right from the start.

INFIDELITY

Dr Christine Munsch looked at survey data regarding infidelity from nearly 10,000 young American adults. She found that a large income disparity heightened the likelihood of cheating. For example, women who earned significantly more money than their partners were more likely to cheat. Equally, men who earned significantly *less or more* than their partners were also more likely to cheat.[107]

The findings set the morality police into overdrive, damning women who try to 'have it all' for risking marital ruin.

Needless to say, this caused a great deal of publicity, as it seemed to suggest high-earning women were doomed to have partners who cheated on them. The amount of media attention this garnered seemed to surprise Dr Munsch herself, who cautioned after the story was picked up by the media: 'We're talking about very small numbers... If you're a woman and you make more money than your partner, your partner isn't 100 per cent likely to cheat.'

The significant conclusion was that infidelity rose when one partner, *male or female*, made a lot more money than the other. Men may lean towards infidelity because they feel a 'gender identity threat by questioning the traditional notion of men as breadwinners,' Munsch speculated.

The media focused on working women's likelihood of being cheated on if a woman had the audacity to out-earn her husband. Scant attention was paid to the fact that high earning men were *also* likely to cheat, almost as if that part was not equally relevant or newsworthy.

'If you work long hours and have more disposable income, it's easier to hide infidelity,' Munsch reasoned. For example, unusual expenses charged to credit cards might go unnoticed. She elaborated: 'People who make more money may also travel frequently and meet lots of people of the opposite sex. As for women, wealth brings them a greater power, whether it's to leave a bad relationship or have an affair.'

In fact, she found the 'safest' amount for women to earn to decrease chances of their husband's infidelity was 75 per cent of his income.[108] This is deemed to be a large enough amount to

---

[107] Munsch, Christin L (2010) 'The Effect of Unemployment and Relative Income Disparity on Infidelity for Men and Women' unpublished manuscript, Cornell University, Ithaca, NY. Presented on 16th August, 2010 in Atlanta, GA at the American Sociological Association's 105th Annual Meeting

[108] Dottinga, R (2010) 'Infidelity rises when she makes more than he does', *Bloomberg Businessweek*, August 16

enable a woman to be financially independent, but not so much that her husband might feel his masculinity was threatened.

In my interviews I did not ask specifically about infidelity, but a few women mentioned it as an issue. Josephine and Pierre went through a difficult patch several years earlier when Josephine found overly-friendly text messages from a female colleague on Pierre's phone, the tone of which made her suspicious of an affair.

She recalls: 'It was a period when I was working all hours. I wasn't home in the evenings and working most weekends too. I took my eye off the ball and I'm sure this girl saw Pierre as a great catch. My intuition tells me that while it was probably not consummated, it was heading down that road.'

How did she react when she first discovered the potential affair? She says: 'When I first found out, I was so furious I drew up a spreadsheet with our respective earnings and showed it to him. I said, "Right, this is how much you are going to live on without me," and he went pale. But the truth is, I need him too; when something doesn't work out for me, I come back to him and cry my eyes out.'

From the tone of her comments, Josephine clearly takes some of the blame for Pierre's near-affair. It weighs on her. Josephine doesn't seem to blame her husband, but says: 'Now as I go into any new period of intense work, it's always in the back of my mind and four years later we are still working through it.' The way she absorbs the blame for his indiscretion indicates that this is a real concern for many working women.

While this couple clearly *loves* each other, they are both working through what it is they *need* about each other. This can be complicated when negotiating from a non-traditional perspective. Pierre needs her financially, and he needs her praise to bolster his confidence. Josephine relies on him psychologically during her down-times and for the effort he puts into maintaining their flexible lifestyle.

The relationship, like most marriages regardless of who is the breadwinner, must be negotiated through a constant state of flux.

SEXUAL TENSION IN THE OFFICE

Working with men where there is sexual tension can become quite tricky for many working women, no matter how much they earn.

One woman, Amelia, who works in a government office, explains: 'When we host events and conferences, I have consciously invited men I knew would be good advocates for me, men who respect me professionally. I have said that my husband was too busy to come when really I didn't invite him. He would have felt awkward in that setting, and truthfully I would have felt awkward too. The few female colleagues I have are married to men who are also civil servants, and my male colleagues are married to women who don't work, so I feel at a double disadvantage.'

While Amelia says she has never had an affair, she admits she's been tempted: 'A male colleague and I are close. I go to him for work-related advice. I'll be honest; he's attractive. But I have resisted *so far.*'

Several of the women had enjoyed career support from their husbands at various stages in their lives. Often as they grew professionally they needed support elsewhere, particularly if they did not feel that their partners were growing in the same direction or facing similar challenges. This type of support can be very attractive, as another woman explains: 'These chaps know me, they know the politics; they know the personalities involved and the obstacles I face.'

Other women mentioned making useful alliances with alpha male colleagues. Leila, an executive in the retail industry, took a close male friend, Robert, to social work events instead of her husband, Ron. She reasoned that Robert made a better advocate for her and was respected by the other men there. Leila says her husband doesn't know. However, I think he may suspect because she also mentioned that Ron dislikes Robert and routinely pokes fun at him.

Similarly, some of the women talked about their male colleagues with a mixture of disdain and admiration. One client, Peggy, who works in telecommunications, says: 'If my husband had been in my industry, I think my career could have been even better. I think he'd relate and could help guide me and leverage what he knows.'

As an executive coach, I often work with plenty of women

who are married to ambitious men in the same industry. The situation can become competitive and is often far from ideal. This is particularly true when a couple has a family and they have to make a decision, unspoken or not, about whose career will take a back seat. More often than not it's the woman's.

When I posed this challenge to her, Peggy relents and agrees: 'Yes, I have a couple of former colleagues who now don't work because their husbands got to be the "big star". They are miserable. I hate it when my male colleagues ignore my husband at the office family day because he stays home part-time. But I'd probably hate it more if they were ignoring me to talk to him just because he was a big shot in another company.'

Maria, a banker, laughs when she tells me about her husband's open disdain for her male colleagues: 'Thank God Elliott is an arrogant bastard. He's confident, which is good because he has to put up with me! He doesn't equate money with success. I'm lucky he's not competitive or jealous of me. He doesn't think he is smarter than *me*, but he doesn't think much of my male colleagues.'

She explains: 'It bothers me at social events because other investment bankers who know what I do will assume that my husband earns the same *or more* than me. When they find out he writes music, there is a moment of surprise, then they completely ignore him. Obviously, he gets annoyed, but he gets his own back. At dinner parties he will run intellectual circles around them, and they have no idea he's actually making fun of them.'

How does he do this? Maria elaborates: 'A lot of the men I work with care only about money and status, even if they didn't grow up with it.' Interestingly, Elliott went to Eton, the esteemed boys' school. She explains: 'We were once in conversation with a couple who were trying to get their son into the school and buying a house in Windsor in preparation. They were fairly dismissive of Elliott at the party. Rather than say he'd gone to the school himself he said, "Well, I guess if you can't get in to Eton, you can always buy the next best thing." I was embarrassed, but I knew exactly where he was coming from. I don't tend to take him to that sort of occasion any more, as it just drags up problems for us.'

At the end of our conversation, Maria says: 'It's a miracle when these types of relationships work. You have to have two very particular personalities: a man who's confident without having the big career and a woman who is *equally* confident without having the big man next to her.'

It is interesting that Maria mentions the two characteristics we have traditionally used to define a person's status. For men it's the career, for women, the man to whom they are attached.

How do they manoeuvre around alpha male colleagues who at times may seem attractive to them? Nancy, who works in investment banking, sighs and explains: 'I'm not attracted to many men I work with, but a few do stand out. They know what they want but they are not corrupted by their talent or greed, which can be a rare combination in my industry! Funnily enough, my husband has those same qualities but perhaps in a different way.'

When asked what keeps her from straying, Nancy says: 'I've been approached by a colleague I admire, and I would be lying if I said I was never tempted, particularly in my dark moments. But fundamentally I'm in love with my husband. No man I have ever met is as *good* as he is. He is an amazing person; he has principles, he's smart, he has strong morals and he's faithful. The men I work with have some of these qualities but not the whole package. My husband is my *rock*.'

Katrina feels similarly and says: 'If Simon wasn't so supportive, I would need a straitjacket. When I look around the office and think of all the kinds of men I could have married, yikes! I couldn't have done it with any of them. I would be more frustrated and feel guilty, neither of which would have helped our relationship.'

How do you feel about the alpha males *you* work with? Is their competitiveness tiresome or a turn-on? Think carefully about the types of men you are attracted to before taking on a female breadwinner role. Equally, have those men been right for you in the past?

Men who earn significantly more or less than their partners may be more likely to cheat.

•

Women who are the primary breadwinners may also be more likely to be unfaithful.

•

Compared to the male colleagues they work with, most women are grateful for their supportive husbands.

Problems Adjusting to the Female Breadwinner Model?

1 Seek relationship help from counsellors or clergy.

2 Talk through re-training or new opportunities for him.

3 Get help from a doctor if depression or substance abuse becomes apparent.

4 Work with your own therapist or coach – women often silence themselves for fear of being disloyal.

9

THE WAY FORWARD

*'A successful marriage requires falling in love
many times, always with the same person.'*
MIGNON MCLAUGHLIN
The Second Neurotic's Handbook

As we have discussed, in any marriage there can be resentment, unspoken hostility and miscommunication. It's no different for male or female breadwinners. However, as we have seen, when there is an issue within a marriage with a female breadwinner, her earnings are not the *cause* of issues, but rather mask other problems. Indeed, as we will now discuss, female breadwinning is a model within which many couples thrive.

So how do they do that? I found that the couples who make an effort to be equitable and not let traditional gender roles define their relationship seem genuinely happier. They are a great source of inspiration and evidence that this type of relationship can work for the benefit of *all* involved.

CHOOSE YOUR PARTNER WISELY

From the work I do with my own clients and the women I interviewed, one thing is clear. Working women, and particularly those who are the main breadwinners, need supportive partners. These partners help them maintain their careers, in much the same way women have historically done for their working husbands.

If there is one message to take away from this book it is this: *choose your partner wisely.* No single other person will be with you day in and day out, through your various roles and in the periods in between jobs. For this reason, supportive husbands are the single most valuable asset a female breadwinner can have.

Indeed, men are increasingly recognising what an asset such an ambitious woman can be. A 2008 study found that men looking for a potential mate increasingly want an educated woman who is a good financial prospect. Women were more interested in a man who wanted a family. This study of undergraduates found that today's young adults ranked love and attraction as the most important factors.

How priorities have changed; in the 1930s those attributes didn't even make the top three.

In the 1930s, men wanted a dependable, kind woman who had skills in the kitchen. Indeed, chastity was deemed more important than intelligence! Twenty-first century men look for love, brains and beauty; the potential to earn a sizable salary increasingly sweetens the deal. Men ranked 'good financial prospect' as number twelve, a significant shift from number eighteen in 1967.[109]

These findings reflect the continued rise in educational and career opportunities for women, and also men's increasing expectation to share financial responsibility with a future partner.

In fact, I believe we don't give modern men the credit they deserve. In researching this book, I met many men who said they would be happy to down-shift their career aspirations to raise children if their wives out-earned them.

One man I talked with, Bill, related a funny story about dating his wife, Dina. In the early days of their relationship, Bill was initially reluctant to bring up his willingness to be at home with future children, since he did not want to be seen as shirking his

---

[109] Whelan, C & Boxer, C (2009) 'Study finds education and money attracts a mate; chastity sinks in importance', University of Iowa press release

duty or taking advantage of his high-earning girlfriend. Ironically, Dina was hugely relieved when they eventually tackled the subject as she hadn't wanted to 'emasculate' him by asking if he was willing to consider this option.

Indeed, I suspect many more men would consider working part-time or giving up work altogether to take care of children, if they were less concerned about how colleagues, friends or even potential partners would react.

SUPPORTIVE HUSBANDS

I found that several husbands of the women I interviewed were willing to make these compromises fairly early on in the relationship. Several women had had conversations about whose career would take a back seat, in some cases several years before she was even pregnant. Other women saw that their future husbands would be supportive long before such questions presented themselves.

By the time Annie, a documentary film maker, met Graham, her second husband, at work, it was clear *she* was considered to be a rising star in the company. Because Graham was younger and had worked at the production company for a short time, they decided within a few months of dating that he should move to another firm. Graham worked as a film editor for other companies for several years, but at the time of our interview had set up his own business outside of the sector.

Annie finds greater empathy in Graham than she did in Jonathan, her first husband, who never understood why she gave so much time and effort to her job. Graham understood how demanding her job could be since he had worked in the same industry.

As we talked, it was apparent that while her two husbands are indeed very different from each other, Annie had also matured from her first marriage in her twenties. Her perspective of what characteristics make a good mate had developed. She explains: 'Graham's incredibly supportive and knows I have to work weekends sometimes and travel. He understands. If I ever complain, he reminds me that we both know what I let myself in for.'

So what does Graham, who works from home but doesn't do any daily childcare, bring to the table? Annie says: 'He's a fantastic guy and very proud of me. The children love him, and he's great at managing our investments. Actually, he is the most brilliant corporate wife. He comes to all the events he needs to, and talks me up to people. He's good-looking and charming as well. He's much better than I would be if the roles were reversed. I'm rubbish at small talk, whereas he can charm anyone.'

Similarly, when I asked Vashti what drew her to her husband, she answers: 'Being with Terence made me realise I had more potential than I gave myself credit for. He encouraged me to apply for my first management position which has shaped my career hugely. He's the first person I talk to about any career issue. He's a great friend and mentor.'

Many of the women were very grateful to their husbands for the support they gave, often commenting that they 'couldn't have done it without him'.

Indeed, many men who stayed at home full-time did so with aplomb and with their sense of confidence and masculinity intact. At my suggestion during our interview that some men find making the shift to primary caregiver difficult, Jackie, a former sale executive, was adamant it wasn't a problem for them. She says: 'Donald's been brilliant. He's never had an issue that I'm the one who brings home the money. He always refers to himself as the "back-up team" to remind me he has things covered. He's my biggest supporter.'

The respect they feel for each other is clear as Jackie elaborates: 'A few years ago, a former boss asked me to take on a big new role. I was sitting at home with Donald when he called and asked, "What will it take for you to accept this job?" Under Donald's encouragement, I threw back a whole list of things I'd love to have but would never get: a steep pay rise, my secretary to come with me, my own corner office. He replied, "You can have them all." I looked at Donald with my hand over the receiver. Donald yelled, "Say yes!" and it was one of the best jobs I ever had.

'I could never have ended up with someone who wasn't supportive of my career. You must make sure you marry the right person.'

To make use of a sporting metaphor, they clearly see themselves as a *winning team*.

LESSONS IN GRATITUDE

Certainly, one theme I heard time and time again was how grateful female breadwinners were to the men in their lives. Merryn Somerset-Webb, Editor of *MoneyWeek*, agrees: 'I do think, for working women, it helps grease the wheels of a relationship if you are grateful. It's hard to imagine the average male ego coping with earning less, or staying home altogether, without some form of verbal gratitude for picking up what is traditionally a female role.

'Just because men have not traditionally shown much gratitude to their wives does not make it the right way! It's better for both sexes to show gratitude for the role they each play in keeping things ticking over.'

Several women say they take pains to remind their partner how grateful they are for his facilitation of her career. It stands to reason that men come to expect this type of 'back-up team' if they are surrounded by male colleagues who have wives who don't work or who are willing to compromise their own career ambitions for the sake of his career. They are just less likely to think about what their partner is giving up to support them.

But women, seeing the relative paucity of support their female colleagues get at home, may be more acutely aware of just how 'lucky' they are. Therefore they are more likely to express the gratitude that may not occur to male colleagues who feel *entitled* to such support.

Not surprisingly, in the happiest couples, gratitude was not one-way traffic; it was expressed towards *each other*. When I speak with Sonia, she and her husband, Neil, had just celebrated their tenth wedding anniversary. They have three children and live outside New York City. When they met, she worked in human resources for an investment bank and earned more than Neil, who worked as an accountant. The year they married, Neil decided to undertake an MBA.

Sonia is sure that Neil would have gone for his MBA whether or not she had earned so well. Even so, she says: 'He was always very grateful to me because of the opportunity. It was a huge investment for us, but so fascinating. It was a difficult time in the markets. There was a lot of downsizing and mergers. He would come home in the evening and talk about the theory he'd learned, and I would match it with what was going on for me at work in the real world. We would talk for hours. It was almost like I got a degree by default!'

At this point the couple had no children, and she speaks animatedly about their ability to talk late into the night about business issues. It clearly was a highlight for both of them, and Sonia bore no resentment about being the only breadwinner for the first several years of their relationship. She got a good deal of intellectual stimulation out of it and viewed it as an *investment* in both of their futures. In fact, she was invited to speak to Neil's classmates several times about career change and the financial services sector, an opportunity she remembers with delight.

It was an auspicious year for the couple, as Sonia became pregnant and gave birth to their first daughter the night before one of Neil's final exams.

What sets Sonia and Neil apart is their open communication style. After the birth, they talked about their future family and who would be the main breadwinner. Neil was clear he soon wanted that role. Sonia was always confident Neil would find a senior job, which he did soon after graduating. Sonia loved her job but wanted to work flexibly, so began her own HR consultancy and their earnings switched.

It's important to note that the discomfort felt by men, as to the value of their contributions, was also characteristic of some of the women who had become accustomed to being the main breadwinner, but who were *no longer* in that role. Sonia smiles as she says: 'When I was establishing my business, it was difficult for me to not bring in the money I used to. It has taken me a long time to be okay with the fact that I don't contribute financially like I used to; I'm probably 95 per cent comfortable with it now. As my business has grown, I take huge pride in anything I can contribute to make it much more even.'

As a society, we value that which can be measured monetarily. Running a household is invisible work since it is not measured economically. It should not be surprising that both men and women question the value of their *non-financial* contributions when this is the primary type of contribution they make. Sonia feels that Neil shows a great deal of gratitude for the time they *both* put in to making their relationship and the family work.

She explains: 'It's in the choices he makes. This year, for example, I have been training for a 10K race. Neil makes sure I have time to run at the weekends. Similarly, he's training for a triathlon. He will say to me, "Thank you so much for having the kids and enabling me to do this." On the day, we will go to watch him which means a lot to us as a family. When he is home, he is fully present. He will help the kids with their homework. He often has dinner with clients in the city and he could stay over but instead he always comes home. He says he wants to wake up next to me and see the kids in the morning.'

There *is* good news for those of us who are not yet this openly appreciative in our marriages. Sonia was clear that this had been a journey; they certainly didn't start the relationship this way. Sonia became more confident in asking for the support she needs as well as verbally thanking Neil for his contributions. This in turn may have encouraged him to do the same.

She explains: 'I used to feel bad about bothering him about my day, after he'd been out all day. And I'd wait until things blew up. Now I'm much more ready to say what I need. I was always putting other people ahead of myself. By bottling things up I wasn't allowing him to be the husband he actually wanted to be. He's great, but he recognises how fundamental *I* am to the running of the household, so he wants me to be in a good place emotionally. We've grown together.'

Sonia is a great example of how wanting more appreciation often starts with *showing* more appreciation.

> *The value in choosing a supportive partner cannot be overestimated.*
>
> •
>
> *Supportive husbands can often serve as an informal coach or mentor.*
>
> •
>
> *Husbands often believe in their female breadwinners more than the women believe in themselves.*

COUPLES WHO SHARE CHORES TOGETHER STAY TOGETHER

As we have seen, husbands are less likely to help around the house if the loss of their breadwinner status is sudden, through illness or unemployment. In these cases, there can be an initial total abdication of all responsibilities around the house, which is compounded by shock, depression, low self-esteem and a sense of victimisation.

Housework can become a major bone of contention, but this does not mean it cannot be managed well. Many of the women I spoke with said their partners picked up the lion's share of housework or childcare to support her breadwinning role. Even couples where both people worked were able to find good ways forward.

My own husband and I share chores. While I'm doing the laundry, he will vacuum. We divide up the work based on which chores we each like – or perhaps I should say, which chores we each dislike the least! We share the cooking, with him preparing four or five dinners a week. *He's* actually the one who inspired me to learn to cook at all.

All this sharing certainly makes the time we spend together more equitable and enjoyable, but I was heartened to hear it might also be a factor in keeping us happier in the long run.

After nineteen years studying more than 50,000 adults in Canada, Rod Beaujot of the University of Western Ontario discovered that the couples who divide chores equally are the happiest. He explained: 'If both parties knuckle down to boring household jobs, couples are less likely to fight over them.'[110] This can only be good news. In fact, the rewards of housework can be even more promising.

Other research found that married couples who spend more hours in housework *and* paid work report the most frequent sex.[111] This group was called the 'work hard, play hard' group by the researchers, who point out: 'Active people tend to pour their energy into *all* pursuits, perhaps making sex a priority.'

Simply put, shared housework can remind people that they are a team and make the couple remember why they got married in the first place. This is certainly on the rise as 72 per cent of people today credit shared chores with helping a happy marriage, up from 47 per cent in 1990.

Being a female breadwinner is not a role most people had modelled to them while they were growing up. Open communication about how it is working, or *not* working, is key. Make sure you have honest discussions about domestic responsibilities. He might assume that because you are a woman you will do the laundry. Likewise, you may think you never have to take out the rubbish. Just because the assumptions are unvoiced doesn't mean they aren't there.

Clearly, sharing childcare and household chores irrespective of gender or breadwinning status worked well for many couples. Jackie, a recently retired retail executive, and her husband, Donald, are a great example of how couples choose to have a stay-at-home partner based on personality rather than gender. They shared in the decision making and chores to get the best results for their family. Having known each other from childhood, they eventually married in their mid-thirties. Jackie trained as a teacher, but felt her earnings and career path were limited. At 28, she decided to move into a marketing role for a department store.

The job she first took wasn't better paid, but as she explains:

---

[110] Beaujot, R (2009) 'Couples who do the dishes together stay happier', *Science Daily*
[111] Gager, C & Yabiku, S (2010) 'Who has the time? The relationship between household labor time and sexual frequency', *Journal of Family Issues*, 31 (2), 135–163

'With teaching, you knew exactly how much of an incremental raise you'd get, and you virtually had to wait for someone to die before any chance of promotion. I'm pretty ambitious and it didn't suit me.'

The company, a major high street retailer, promoted her several times in just a few years. Jackie says: 'I never consciously thought, *this project will get me to the top*. I just said yes to opportunities others weren't willing to take on. I once heard a woman at a conference saying she allowed herself to see sex discrimination one day a year. I thought that was a good mantra. I've always tried to just get on with things. I knew sexism existed, particularly when I started out in the early seventies, but I didn't focus on it.'

GETTING COMFORTABLE WITH DELEGATION

One of the most important things a woman could do to get more done around the house and make her partner feel needed was to delegate. This seems obvious, but for most working women delegation is a real challenge.

High-achieving women have often got to the positions they have because of high standards that they feel only they can achieve. However, just like at the office, not delegating will cause far more problems in the long run. Women had to let go of feeling that as 'good' wives and mothers, they had to do it all.

After setting up my business, hiring a cleaner was the first type of support I got. At the time, I struggled to justify the cost to myself. I believed that if I hired someone to help me in this area, I would use those extra four hours per week to work on business development. Plus I lost the 'guilt time' I experienced whilst berating myself that the house wasn't always spick and span.

Our cleaner was able to do in four hours chores that would have taken my husband and me an entire Saturday every few weeks. Oddly, her presence also drives the inner guilt in me to be even more productive in the hours while she is dusting and scrubbing.

I am not alone. You don't have to be superwoman; ask for what you need. Allison laughs: 'We manage quite well, but there had to be more discussion after Alexander was born. There's just so much more to do! In the end we created a chart which labelled out everything that needs to get done. I think we do fifty-fifty. We share what needs to be done in the morning, and George probably cooks more than I do. But I do all the laundry, feeding Alexander and getting him ready for bed. George stepped up when the baby was born because it became obvious how knackered I was when I was falling asleep by 7pm, trying to do it all myself. It wasn't that George refused to help; I felt I had to do it all myself to make up for the fact I can't be with him during the day.'

Ask yourself: what will make the biggest difference to your quality of life – emotional support, more housework, more time spent with the children? You may not get exactly what you want. But you certainly won't if you don't ask. What are the three household tasks that make the biggest difference to the way you feel?

If your partner is not immediately keen on this idea, you could try explaining that you and he need to spend more time together, and this would also mean you will be less stressed with him. Ask him what you can do together to make things easier for both of you.

GIVING UP CRITICISM

Other women found they created perfectionist standards that no one else could maintain – nor did anyone else have any interest in maintaining them.

Maria explains: 'It's only been recently that I started to relinquish control. I used to ask Elliott to do things but then didn't like the way he did them so I would take over. I started out organising everything, even though I work long hours and he works from home. Finally, I realised I had created the exact situation that I resented! Now Elliott handles all aspects of their after-school music lessons for the children because he cares more than I do about that, and he also organises our annual Christmas holidays. I had to delegate them and just get over it. The kids also remind him of things so I don't always have to.'

Maria's eventual willingness to delegate benefited the relationship hugely. Elliott now does more cooking and house maintenance. At the weekends, she encourages him to go camping and motorbiking with friends. Interestingly, she notices that since she relinquished control, he has wanted to do more *with* her. In fact, she says that she feels the relationship is in the best shape it has been in for years.

What was vital for Maria, and other women in this situation, was to change her perspective. She explains: 'For years I used to think that being the main breadwinner was a condition imposed on me, but I now realise that as much as I love my children, I am not a full-time mum. It's forced me to grow my career, which suits me better anyway.'

Other women struggled with the transition to asking for help and *allowing* their partner to step up to the plate. Grace runs her own PR company and is married to Dan, a cabinet maker. They always knew her business had the real earning potential. In their early days with children, she wanted to retain control of the day-to-day running of the house, even whilst she was travelling for work.

She explains: 'I would call up from a client's office and in addition to asking how they all were, would question Dan about his handling of the logistics. I questioned him on how the children were getting to activities, what they were eating everything. I found that, as a mother, you don't get away from feeling responsible no matter where you are or how capable your partner is. Needless to say, he clearly felt I was barking orders down the phone. We had to talk about what we each brought to the family. I'm very organised, but he actually manages the house and children very well, so now I leave all of that to him.'

To streamline their lives even more, Grace and Dan eventually sold their rambling big house for a smaller modern house. She explains: 'We both wanted to sleep easier at night without thinking about the bills and what needed fixing next.'

In many marriages, spouses do have different standards of housekeeping. If both partners work, standards will be hard to meet, at least not without major exhaustion. As a couple you must share authority and expertise. If he's home all day with the kids, you can't complain he's not doing the dishes *the right way*. He doesn't come into your office criticising your reports.

Certainly, both partners in these relationships need to contribute domestically, but if it is a question of style over substance, you may have to grit your teeth and bear it. Plus, taking on all housework yourself only serves your husband. How likely is anyone to offer to help, when their contributions are met only with criticism? Indeed, if you take it all on, many men would think the price of a resentful wife is worth the benefit of not having to lift a finger themselves. If not addressed, this can lead to a destructive cycle of blame, isolation, accusation and frustration.

I once had a client, Miranda, who realised in a session where she was discussing her frustrations at home, that the *way* the laundry was folded was less important to her than the fact that it was folded at all. Unless you are not getting the amount of help you need, criticising the efforts your partner makes to help can upset the balance of power in a marriage.

Alternatively, you could use some of that extra income to pay for housecleaning, or cooking, childcare or gardening, or whatever task causes the most arguments.

As I discuss in *Beyond the Boys' Club*, just as in a well-run office, you will have to let go of some of your perfectionist tendencies in return for two main benefits. The first is that you don't have to do everything, and the second is that your husband does not feel he is always being criticised about what he is doing wrong. Isn't that worth a dusty coffee table or two?

The Six Rules for a Happier Home Life

1   Ask for help you need.

2   Don't criticise his efforts at helping.

3   Make deadlines, but don't step in if those deadlines are missed.

4   Lower your expectations.

5   Use cash to get the domestic help you need.

6   Show gratitude.

7   Remind him shared chores make for a better sex life.

HOW SHOULD MONEY BE MANAGED?

As we have seen in the chapter 'Dirty, Sexy Money', couples with female breadwinners, like other types of families, use a variety of systems to manage their income.

In an exploratory study of female breadwinners, women on the whole did not enjoy a disproportionate amount of power in financial management. Rather, many women conceded power to the man, which minimised her power opportunities but increased her sense of responsibility and worry associated with the role.[112]

I also found most women took pains to make their partner feel completely equal in all money matters, even if it was at a cost to their own understanding of their finances. This is likely to be a reaction to the way money has historically been used to control women, as the lower-earning spouse. Women were sensitive about being seen as *controlling* when it came to money. Perhaps they recognised that because money was a tool they had

---

[112] Stamp, P (1985) 'Balance of financial power in marriage: An explanatory study of breadwinning wives', *Sociological Review*, 33, 546–557

at their disposal, they did not want to be seen to wield it more than necessary.

So, why do so many high-earning women allow their husbands, whether they stay at home or not, to control all aspects of the investments? Several women simply said their partners had more time to manage the money. While time certainly may be a factor, I suspect there is more to it than that. Historically, busy working men rarely handed over the investment portfolio to their stay-at-home wives on the grounds that they had 'more time'.

Merryn Somerset-Webb, editor of *Moneyweek* and author of *Love is Not Enough* agrees: 'I think it's about confidence. Women don't necessarily want to manage the money, and men don't necessarily want to let go of it. Women haven't been raised to be confident with the skill, and even if men aren't earning any more or are no more financially savvy than their wife, it gives them power they may not feel in other areas.'

She elaborates: 'He may not take international business trips like she does, but he can decide if the family will be investing in China or India this year. Plus, I think most men show an interest in money management because they start with the assumption they will support a family. When a man walks down the aisle, I don't think it ever occurs to him he might be the person at home, with his wife supporting him. Men think it will be their responsibility and often take the lead on money matters accordingly.'

It leads to the question, how exactly should couples handle money?

Merryn advocates what could conceivably be the fairest way to distribute money between a couple. She explains: 'Lots of families run a joint account, but they do it in a variety of ways. Let's say she earns £3,000 a month and he earns £2,400. They might each put £2000, the same absolute amount, into a joint account to cover their basics. The problem is this leaves her with a discretionary £1,000 to spend on clothes or whatever she wants but it only leaves him with £400 extra to spend on his personal needs.'

She continues: 'Alternatively, some might think the answer is to have the lesser paid person do all of their personal spending out of the joint account, but that's not a great solution either. He will feel he has to account for each expenditure, and report it to her. There is never a sense of it being *our* money, but *her* money since she is the one bringing it in.'

Certainly this model does have its problems as it makes the person earning less feel beholden to the other and that everything must be constantly re-negotiated. Merryn's solution? All money goes into one pot, but then each person gets a certain *absolute* amount in a separate account for their discretionary spending. Each person having the same amount of spending money would be the fairest way forward, and as Merryn argues: 'It would be a huge step towards marital equality.'

How should couples, where one partner is self-employed and with fluctuating earnings, manage? This was cited as a reason many husbands could not be expected to contribute financially.

Merryn again suggests that no matter what the income disparity, both partners get the same absolute amount to spend at their own discretion. The same applies if only one person is working for pay.

'If you are in a relationship where money is discussed openly and regularly, then it doesn't matter if one person's contributions have to change because of the vagaries of self-employment. The problems only arise in relationships regarding money if things are hidden and not discussed. A system should be flexible. The point is not to create rigidity but a secure and transparent base to family finances so you both know what's going on.'

Merryn continues: 'I feel so strongly that money should be joint. What's the point of earning well if you have no idea where it is going? I think it is perfectly reasonable for the stay-at-home partner to oversee all aspects of the money from budgeting to investing. They still need to talk about it and go through statements every few months. It all leads back to communication. It needs to be an ongoing conversation; schedule meetings even! I understand that women want to massage his ego, but that's no excuse to give all the control away. The problem is when people of either gender become *dependent via ignorance*.'

Interestingly, several of the husbands had placed themselves in the same precarious position many women have historically been in, neither earning nor understanding where the money is going.

Clearly, as we saw earlier, a lack of honesty and transparency over finances can lead to devastating problems in any relationship. Merryn elaborates: 'Money is one of the leading causes of divorce and even suicide. Money underpins pretty much every source of unhappiness there is. It can't buy happiness, but a lack of it can make you pretty unhappy.

'As a couple, you need to be clear on your financial priorities and what can be taken out of joint spending, and what can't. These can be long conversations about *needs* versus *wants*, but the unspoken resentment that can build if you don't talk is far worse. Financial honesty and trust is the basis on which romantic love can thrive. It can be dashed in seconds with an unexpected credit card bill.'

Accept that you will have to drive financial discussions. You can share in financial decisions, but it will probably be you who initiates such discussions, orchestrates your financial future and monitors how the money is organised.

Sharing Finances the Right Way

If he works, you each contribute to the joint account as you can, but you allocate an absolutely equal amount for spending.

•

Set up two separate discretionary accounts in addition to your joint account for all the basic bills.

•

Upgrade your life insurance and disability cover. If he is a full-time stay-at-home father, you may be able to do away with his policies completely as children are unlikely to be financially reliant on him.

•

Address his retirement savings. If he's staying home with the kids, invest in a personal pension and ISAs. If he's working at all, make sure he contributes to his employer's pension plan.

•

Schedule time for talks about money and look at written figures. Label it in black and white, such as outstanding bills and savings goals. Talk about where exactly the money is.

10

FINAL THOUGHTS ON MOVING FORWARD AS A FEMALE BREADWINNER

'Marriage is like twirling a baton, turning a handspring or eating with chopsticks; it looks so easy until you try it.'

HELEN ROWLAND
Reflections of a Bachelor Girl (1909)

If there is a basic starting point for high-earning women who might become primary breadwinners, it is to choose your partner carefully.

Ask yourself and your partner where you want to be in five, ten, twenty years. What do you want to achieve in life? Sure, answers may change, but you will get a sense of what his version of success includes and what it doesn't, which can be very telling and a great starting point for discussions. Look for someone who does not see your success as a slight on their own achievements.

One of the best things female breadwinners can do is to check the arrangement is still working for *both* of you.

People who feel trapped or resentful by being the main breadwinner are those for whom it ceases to be a choice, but rather is an expectation. Remain flexible, and focus on what works *now*. Just as many of the women I interviewed became the main breadwinner by circumstance rather than design, your situation may change again. These roles are fluid; most couples had experienced a mix of him being the main breadwinner, them both earning equally, and her being the breadwinner, at different stages in their relationship. The situation now may not last forever. Being open to change allows you both to make the most of what you have *right now*.

Making sure partners felt some type of personal satisfaction was key.

If your partner works, find out what he loves about his job. If he is a stay-at-home partner, encourage him to play sport or volunteer his talents in your local community. People with only one role are most likely to feel stifled by any job, no matter how much they initially love it. Be sensitive to his ambition. Even if you are dubious, encourage him to set goals around activities he enjoys. Running a marathon, setting up a website, taking on a leadership role within your children's school all are great goals. We all like to feel we are achieving things.

Many of the happiest women were humble enough to realise that their value was not determined by the size of their pay packet. It takes humility to realise that just because you are exponentially earning more does not mean you are exponentially more important to the family. Similarly, your partner is no less important to the family just because he earns less, if anything at all.

Gratitude was one of the simplest, yet often overlooked, actions in a partnership.

While husbands historically have taken a smoothly running home for granted, the smartest female breadwinners do not. They show gratitude verbally, but also by making sure he has time to do things for himself. Just as many women feel underappreciated at work, home life is seldom better.

How frequently do you thank your partner for the difference he makes in your life? If you feel you do not hear it enough yourself, be the change you want to see, and practise what you preach. If you struggle with gratitude after coming home to a kitchen full of dirty dishes, ask yourself: 'Am I better served by him being here or if he was working full-time like me?' If the answer surprises you, it may be time for a discussion.

I AM A FEMALE BREADWINNER,
HEAR ME ROAR

On the whole, I was heartened by the stories I heard from the female breadwinners I met.

Certainly, some faced major challenges within their relationships. What is important to remember is that I could have interviewed women who earned the same as, or less than, their partners and found a variety of *other* challenges. Many women faced both highs and lows in their relationships, and were able to successfully and proudly reconcile with the role of female breadwinner.

What woman or man doesn't resent their partner at times? What woman is sure she has got it all figured out? What man doesn't want to be contributing to the success of their family? These are issues we all have to face, no matter who brings home the bacon.

In the end, I think the story of Maureen and Bill is a good example of a couple who had faced perhaps more than their fair share of highs and lows, but who were still willing to work through it. On the whole their relationship, and her breadwinning, *worked for them.*

When Maureen was building her PR business, Bill was very supportive. As it grew, however, his support waned. She says: 'We had a party to celebrate the tenth anniversary of the business. I could sense his resentment growing. I think he got sick of hearing how great I was from other people.'

How does this manifest itself? She sighs: 'On his down days, Bill will say I care about my business more than the family. He'll complain he's tired of playing second fiddle. He knows I won't really retaliate because it's not in my nature. He'll get broody for weeks, and then when I finally ask, "What the hell's wrong with you?" he'll give me both barrels, like it's been waiting to come out.'

Historically, Maureen avoided conflict with Bill. She credits her new willingness to stand up for herself as part of the reason they are now getting on better. She explains: 'Obviously if there is a real issue we discuss it, but I take his moods less personally now, and just tell him when I don't agree. I'm not willing to feel guilty any longer.' By denying him an audience when he wants to provoke her, she defuses the situation.

Things came to a head a few years ago, the day before a press release Bill was due to write was needed for a client. Bill told Maureen he no longer wanted to write the piece and that she'd have to find someone else. In previous years, she would have spent the extra hours writing it herself and stewing about his last-minute refusal. Instead, she says: 'I just looked at him, and said, "Bill, I never have that choice. There are plenty of things I don't want to do, but I just have to get on with it. You don't have that choice either; this is *our* livelihood."'

Ironically, when Bill eventually wrote the piece he was given a particularly favourable compliment from the client. She adds: 'It sounds awful, but I was so angry because he was potentially messing with my brand. I would be horrified if my company failed to deliver on a project. I've worked too hard to build this up.' Even so, Maureen recognises that giving him one-off pieces of writing has directly contributed to his self-confidence.

Maureen remarks: 'There certainly has been an undercurrent of tension between us. We've only arrived at a good place in the last few years. We both accept our roles and respect our strengths and weaknesses. It's brought a calmness to life. There's not a lot of respect for stay-at-home dads or men who take the supporting role. Men have to get their kudos from somewhere. If you're like my husband, where do you get your kudos from?'

Where *does* Bill get his sense of self-satisfaction? She answers: 'He is very proud when people in our village talk about something he wrote in our local paper. At the moment, we are refurbishing our kitchen. As much as I would love to hire a team of people to finish it in a few weeks, I put up with it taking months so that Bill can say "I did that."'

Maureen tells me a story I think has probably also reduced Bill's resentment over his supporting role. She says: 'He used to hedge his answers if other men asked him what he did because he was embarrassed. Last year, a couple of men responded with variations of "you lucky bastard!" when he finally told them about his mix of DIY, writing and spending time with Sarah. I think that's changed his perception somewhat.'

External validation for his lifestyle, particularly from *men* he respects, enhances his own sense of self-worth. She adds: 'Plus, he's nearly 50, and your version of success changes as you get older. You focus on how you *want* to spend your time. Perhaps he realises he doesn't have such a bad gig after all!'

Indeed, in many cases, I saw more acceptance of a breadwinning wife as men aged. I think this may be for three main reasons. In the first instance, I suspect older men are less preoccupied with their own career success and less likely to see their wives' accomplishments as threats to their own masculinity. Secondly, older men may be more confident about the contributions they have *already* made, and if they are ready to wind down professionally they can see the value in family time and a comfortable sense of balance.

Lastly, the longer a couple is together, it stands to reason that the quality of their relationship and their likely acceptance of each other improves with time. All of these mean that older men may be more accepting of their wife's role as primary breadwinner.

My own husband is older than me and talks openly about fostering my success as he winds down his own career over the next ten years. Initially I felt daunted by the change. After researching this book, however, I now see good signs in both our communication style and his current willingness to take on an equal share of the housework. He has outside interests in sport and in the community that I know will provide him with opportunities to grow after we have switched roles. He has always been extremely supportive of my work and sees our success as shared. He also enjoys the time we have together and is very house-proud – just like me.

I am optimistic we will make the transition as successfully as many other couples.

Maureen and Bill have definitely had their share of difficult years. Maureen, however, is determined to make the relationship work and is clearly seeing the benefits of this decision. She explains: 'I'm a great believer in working at something. If you switch partners, you often keep repeating your mistakes. No matter how in love you are, I think every relationship gets to a point where it will need a huge amount of work. You can either do the work together or leave and have to learn the same old lessons with new partners.'

As Maureen wisely points out: 'Isn't it easier just to make it work? The good thing is that I think we are heading in the right direction now.' While at times she may resent aspects of Bill's 'easier' lifestyle, Maureen knows that taking a secondary status role is not that 'easy' for him. More importantly, she knows it is not a role she would want for herself. I think Maureen speaks for the female breadwinners I met when she says: 'I may complain at times, but I like to know I can rely on myself.' Like most of the other women, Maureen knows being a female breadwinner is the *right* role for her now, and is not one she would opt out of even if given the choice.

Download your
FREE
Career Savvy Checklist

For Female Breadwinners to develop
your career and your relationship

VISIT
http://femalebreadwinners.com/savvy-checklist/

NOTES

NOTES

NOTES

NOTES

NOTES

NOTES

ABOUT THE AUTHOR

Dr Suzanne Doyle-Morris received her PhD from the University of Cambridge where she explored the experiences of successful women in male dominated fields. She is regular speaker to corporate audiences and has worked with clients at Morgan Stanley, Barclays, Unilever, Clifford Chance, Accenture, Deloitte, Microsoft, Ernst and Young, BP, University of Cambridge, St. Andrew's University, Trinity College Dublin and the Sanger Centre.

Her specialism is in helping female professionals succeed, particularly in traditionally male-dominated industries. She is a fellow of the Professional Speakers Association and accredited with the International Coach Federation. She speaks regularly for external networks such as Women in Technology, Women in Banking and Finance, Women in Wealth, Women on the Wharf and Business Women of Scotland among others.

Dr. Doyle-Morris is also the author of *Beyond the Boys' Club: Strategies for Achieving Career Success as a Woman Working in a Male Dominated Field* and is regularly interviewed for publications such as the *Times*, *Telegraph*, *Glamour* and *Stylist* magazines. An Australian-born, American expatriate, she currently lives in the East Neuk of Scotland with her husband. For more support for female breadwinners or information on having Dr. Doyle-Morris speak at your event, workshops, coaching and webinars please visit **www.femalebreadwinners.com**.

Lightning Source UK Ltd.
Milton Keynes UK

177471UK00004B/6/P